More Lancashire MURDERS

ALAN HAYHURST

The History Press

First published 2011

The History Press
The Mill, Brimscombe Port
Stroud, Gloucestershire, GL5 2QG
www.thehistorypress.co.uk

British Library Cataloguing in Publication Data.
A catalogue record for this book is available from the British Library.

ISBN 978 0 7524 5645 4

Typesetting and origination by The History Press
Printed in Great Britain

CONTENTS

ACKNOWLEDGEMENTS

The author wishes to thank the following: Matilda Richards and the team at The History Press; Perry Bonewell, of Bolton Archives Department; the staff of the 'Weaver's Cottage', Rawtenstall; Paula Bradbury, Ronnie and the rest of the team at Whitworth Historical Society; John Ogan; Alan Godfrey Maps; Elaine at Cemsearch; Diana Rushton at Blackburn-with-Darwen Community History Department; the staff of Manchester Central Library; Salford Local History Library; the National Archives, Kew. As always, my best thanks are to my wife for her invaluable assistance, driving, proofreading and, not least, for fitting in with my erratic comings and goings and variable mealtimes.

ALSO BY THE AUTHOR

Cheshire Murders
Greater Manchester Murders
Lancashire Murders
Staffordshire Murders

INTRODUCTION

As I mentioned in the introduction to *Lancashire Murders*, my first book for The History Press in their *True Crime History* series, Lancashire seems to have had more than its fair share of notorious crimes, and my research for the present volume certainly bears this out. Whilst it must always be born in mind that each and every murder is a tragedy for at least two people and often, sadly, many more, I have tried to find a novel twist in every tale, to relieve the monotony of the blunt instrument and the cut-throat razor, which seemed to occur with startling regularity in the nineteenth and early twentieth centuries.

Once again, I have taken the liberty of treating Lancashire in its original form, before the waters became muddied after the administrative reorganisation in the early seventies, so that although Merseyside and Greater Manchester are now counties in their own right, they are still both included in the County Palatinate of Lancaster, and so are entitled to be included in this book.

Wherever possible, I have avoided putting words into the mouths of the people mentioned in this book, preferring to rely on newspaper accounts, verbatim reports of the trials and the voluminous files of the National Archives for my information. I have also been fortunate enough to come across people who had personal recollections and who were willing to discuss them with me. In several cases, I have used the Freedom of Information Act 2002 to obtain files from the National Archives which have not been released to the public before, and was also able to point out to Kew that one file had been given the wrong name over a hundred years ago and so had effectively remained hidden until I discovered it.

1

SUSPICIOUS DEATH IN THE WORKHOUSE

Oldham, 1887

The Victorian workhouse was not designed for comfort. The poor were a drag on the finances of the community, and the Guardians took good care to make sure that only the very deserving were given anything in the nature of a cash handout. The indolent and those who could not work for reasons of health, age or infirmity performed primitive tasks for little recompense, apart from three meals a day and a roof over their heads. Husbands were separated from wives, children from their parents and the workhouse was rightly regarded as the last resort of the desperate, although it was the inmate's privilege to sign himself out of the workhouse if he wished. Many who did, however, soon returned.

The inmates wore something akin to a prison uniform. The food, although adequate, had often little nourishment in it and varied from establishment to establishment. Discipline was strict and children under fourteen could be flogged, but each workhouse had its own infirmary where some attempt was made to look after the sick.

One such workhouse was at Rochdale Road, Oldham, built in 1848 and completed three years later. It was here that thirty-one-year-old Elizabeth Berry worked as a hospital nurse on a salary of £25 per annum, about the same pay as a housemaid in service. A widow, Elizabeth had borne two children, one of which died in infancy and the survivor, eleven-year-old Edith Annie, was lodged with her sister-in-law, Mrs Ann Sanderson, at 68 Albion Street, Miles Platting, Manchester. Elizabeth paid 3s a week for her child's maintenance, sixpence a week for schooling and a penny for insurance. She also paid for Edith's clothing, so this did not leave Elizabeth much for her own needs out of her pay of less than 10s a week. Even so, her position at the workhouse was quite comfortable and she even had the luxury of two 'servants', inmates of the workhouse who were presumably given some small reward for looking after their mistress.

Mrs Elizabeth Berry from a contemporary print. (Author's collection)

On 27 December 1886, Elizabeth visited the Sandersons and when she returned to the workhouse on the 29th, she brought with her Edith and the child's friend and companion, thirteen-year-old Beatrice Hall, who Edith had met at Sunday School. At the time, both girls were in good health and were well nourished, although Edith was not very robust. Elizabeth had invited them both to spend their Christmas holidays at Oldham and, despite their unprepossessing surroundings, the two children played happily within the confines of the workhouse, supervised by Elizabeth, the three all sleeping together in Elizabeth's bed.

The hospital part of the workhouse was divided into several blocks and Elizabeth had her sitting room in one block and her bedroom in another. Next to the sitting room was the surgery, where the various drugs used by the medical advisor were kept. Some of these drugs were naturally of a poisonous nature, but Elizabeth had access to the room at all times and could come and go as she pleased.

At about half past nine on the morning of 1 January 1887, a woman named Dillon saw young Edith going from her mother's bedroom to the sitting room, seemingly in her usual good health. Three quarters of an hour later Dillon saw the girl in the surgery with her mother, and at 10.45 a.m. she found Edith in the sitting room, vomiting copiously. As she entered the room, Dillon saw that Edith had a tumbler of liquid in her hand and was saying to Elizabeth, 'Oh mother, I can't drink it.'

Another inmate of the workhouse, Alice Allcroft, (one of Elizabeth's 'servants'), said later that she had earlier been sent by Mrs Berry into the surgery, which at the time was unlocked, for a box of powders that Alice thought were used to make fizzy drinks. Some time later, another workhouse assistant, Ellen Thompson, saw Edith still vomiting and on Elizabeth's instructions busied herself mopping up the vomit, which was thrown away. Time passed and Edith was no better, so Dr Patterson, the workhouse surgeon, was sent for. He prescribed a mixture of iron and quinine and Edith was taken to her mother's bedroom, where she remained in the same state and showing no improvement as the day went on. That night Elizabeth nursed her daughter, allowing no-one else to take over this task, and next morning Dr Patterson found Edith much better and told Elizabeth that he was hopeful that she would make a full recovery. He was given one of the towels into which the girl had vomited and noticed that it had a decidedly acid smell.

Frontage of the Oldham workhouse. (Courtesy of Peter Higginbottom)

About two o'clock that afternoon, Ellen Thompson stole into the room to snatch a look at the child, who was now sleeping, and as she bent over the bed she noticed a blister on the child's upper lip. Just then, Elizabeth came in and Thompson pointed this out. 'Oh,' said Elizabeth, 'I have been giving her orange and sugar, so I suppose it's the orange that has done that.' This explanation satisfied Thompson and she carried on with her duties, whilst Elizabeth remained with her daughter. In the late afternoon Sarah Anderson, Head Nurse of the Female Imbecile Ward, came into the room and spent several minutes talking to the girl's mother. She saw that the child looked very ill, but did not notice any blistering round her mouth, although she did see it when she visited her again on the Monday. Late in the evening Dr Patterson came in with another doctor and they found Edith very much worse than when he had last seen her. The two medical men spent several minutes discussing the child's symptoms and decided that a dose of morphia and bismuth might alleviate her sufferings, but they also agreed between themselves that she seemed unlikely to recover.

Edith continued to be sick all that night and the following morning; Elizabeth gave her daughter some whitish medicine, which she could not, or would not, keep down. 'She cannot take it,' Elizabeth said to Ellen Thompson, 'Her throat is made up.' The girl continued to decline on the following day, Monday, and eventually died at 5 a.m. on Tuesday 4 January.

After she died, her mother was heard saying that she had no insurance for the girl and that she would have to pay all the funeral expenses herself. However, on 6 January, Elizabeth visited an insurance company who paid her the sum of £10.

Unbeknown to Elizabeth, however, the doctors now suspected foul play and Dr Patterson went to see the Chief Constable of Oldham, Charles Hodgkinson, with his

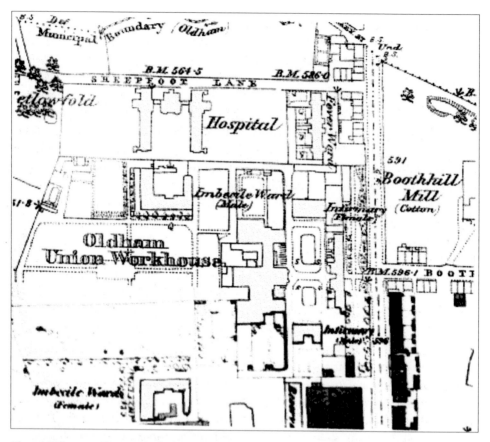

Plan of Oldham workhouse. (Author's collection)

suspicions. This resulted in a visit from the Chief Constable to the workhouse, where he was shown into Elizabeth's sitting room; she was told that he had come to enquire into the death of her daughter who, it was reported, had died suddenly. 'Very well,' was her reply and the Chief Constable followed her into the bedroom where the corpse was lying with a cloth over its face. The Chief Constable removed it carefully and bent down to examine the marks on the dead girl's lips and chin. Straightening up, he told Elizabeth bluntly that the doctors believed that her daughter had been poisoned. The bereaved mother made no reply.

In response to questioning by the Chief Constable, Elizabeth said that her sister-in-law, Mrs Sanderson, had told her that Edith was suffering from constipation and that when she gave the girl a pill, she always passed blood. She went on to say that when her daughter arrived at the workhouse a week ago, she had been unwell, but had had no medicine other than what the doctor had given her, and even that she had been unable to keep down.

'What about the blistering round her mouth?' asked Hodgkinson.

'Well, her mouth was ulcerated when she came to the workhouse,' was the reply, 'So I suppose that must be the cause. I've never seen a mouth like it before.'

In view of the circumstances, Elizabeth was told that there would have to be a coroner's inquest and a post-mortem, to which she reluctantly agreed. The inquest began on 7 January before Coroner Frederick Nassau Molesworth, who, together with the jury, viewed the dead girl's body before the proceedings started. The first witness was Ann Sanderson, who said that the dead girl had lived with her and her husband for five years, after her father had died and her mother had given up the house and sought work as a nurse. Edith and her friend had gone to Oldham with her mother on 29 December and she had heard nothing more of her until she received a telegram at ten in the morning on 3 January saying, 'Come at once, Edith is dying. L. Berry, Oldham Union Workhouse.'

She immediately went to Oldham with her husband and saw the ailing child in her mother's room. 'Whatever is the matter?' she asked Elizabeth, who replied, 'It is acute stoppage of the bowels.'

'However did that come about?' Ann asked.

'Well, she had a good supper and I think that might have been the cause,' replied Elizabeth. This was, of course, nonsense in medical terms, but everyday medicine was still primitive in the extreme at that time, and Mrs Sanderson had probably not the first idea whether Elizabeth was talking sense or not; after all, the girl's mother was a nurse. She did, however, notice that the girl's mouth was sore and blistered.

Mrs Sanderson said that she had remained at the workhouse until the girl died, and saw that she had tried to drink a little tea and also some soda water, but brought it back each time, streaked with blood. Three injections of milk were given towards the end, but nothing could save Edith. About an hour before the child died Elizabeth left the room, saying that she could not bear to see her daughter die. In reply to a question from the coroner, Ann Sanderson said that she believed the dead girl had been insured with the Rational Insurance Office, in the sum of £13. She also told the hearing that Elizabeth had asked her for the insurance card and said that she was going to draw the money.

On 6 January, a post-mortem examination was made on the body by pathologist Thomas Harris, and he told the inquest that he had noticed the blistering, although the tongue and the mucous membrane of the mouth were both normal. At the junction of the middle and lower oesophagus there was a circular patch, which had the appearance of being black and corroded, about an inch in diameter. He also noticed a large number of small ecchymoses (bruises) on the stomach lining. Certain organs had been removed and sent to the Manchester City Analyst.

Young Beatrice Hall told the inquest how she and Edith had gone to the workhouse and had enjoyed themselves, one day going into Oldham and each buying a pennyworth of chocolate. On the Friday evening they went to bed as usual, and by 9 a.m. the next morning Beatrice was up and eating her breakfast. Edith complained of being sick and that was the first time, Beatrice said, that she noticed her friend was ill. Mrs Berry had given her daughter a seidlitz powder, which Edith was able to swallow easily and, later on, some ice, but so far as she could recall Edith had no solid food after supper on Friday. Late on Saturday afternoon she had gone into the bedroom to find Edith alone. She read to her for a while and exchanged a few words, then Edith bade her 'Goodnight' in a weak voice. Beatrice thought that her friend was just a little better than she had been earlier in the day.

Ellen Thompson told the inquest that she had seen the two children playing in the corridors, and on Saturday morning they looked happy enough, but by 11 a.m. Edith was sitting on her mother's knee, head against her shoulder, and was vomiting frequently. Elizabeth said that it was most probably a bilious attack, and when Ellen offered to sit up with the child Elizabeth refused, saying she would do it herself. By Sunday morning, when she saw Edith again, Ellen thought that she looked a little better. At around two o'clock, she went into the bedroom and Elizabeth told her that Dr Patterson had gone for a physician.

'You know what that means,' she said darkly to Ellen. 'My girl was nothing to begin with and being weakly, is not likely to recover.'

Receipt of this news does not seem to have affected Ellen Thompson very much, but then infant mortality was normal in late Victorian times and most families saw one or more children die in infancy. Unsanitary conditions, malnutrition and poor medical techniques contributed to the death toll.

The inquest was then adjourned to 20 January, when it continued with Dr Charles Estcourt, the Manchester City Analyst, describing his examination of the organs sent to him, saying that all were either alkaline or neutral: 'There was no free acid present in any of the organs,' he told the inquest. He had tested for sulphuric acid and found only a trace, which he said could have been due to natural causes. Further tests had proved negative and at the end of his evidence he said: 'The remains were examined for metallic and organic compounds, with the result that none were found. I found nothing that would account for death in any way.'

Considering that Elizabeth was virtually standing before the coroner's jury on trial for her life, this was important evidence in her favour. Various other witnesses told their stories and, once the evidence was completed, Mr Molesworth said to Elizabeth: 'Having heard the evidence, do you wish to say anything?'

'No,' was the reply. The coroner's jury, as they were entitled to at that time, then brought in a verdict of 'Murder' against her and she was remanded to the next Assizes.

The trial lasted four days, during which Mr Justice Hawkins and the jury were told that although the accused had protested that her daughter was uninsured, and so she would have to pay all the funeral expenses herself, she had in fact drawn £10 from the Rational Insurance Office, and in the April before the girl's death she had tried to persuade a company to insure her and her daughter jointly for the sum of £100, payment to go to the survivor. However, the directors of the insurance company concerned had not accepted this proposal, although Elizabeth had not been told of this at the time of the child's death.

The medical evidence at the trial was conflicting. Analyst Charles Estcourt stuck to his guns, repeating that he had found no direct poison in the remains, but Dr Patterson was adamant that a corrosive poison, most likely sulphuric acid, had

Mock-up of an execution from a postcard, c. 1911. (Author's collection)

James Berry. (Author's collection)

been given and had caused the blistering round the dead girl's mouth. He said that the poison must have been administered on the Saturday or Sunday morning, so that by Tuesday, the day of her death, no trace would have been found in the body. Whether this statement would have been left unchallenged in a modern court-room is doubtful.

Given the state of medical knowledge at the time, and the poor quality of the prosecution evidence, Mrs Berry was unfortunate that Dr Estcourt's evidence was not given greater weight by the jury, who brought in a verdict of 'Murder'. Elizabeth was promptly sentenced to death.

Almost certainly, it was the disclosure in court that she had attempted to insure her daughter for £100 and the initial denial that she had had any insurance at all, that was her downfall.

The hangman was her namesake, James Berry, who had actually known his victim slightly, having danced with her at a police ball some years before. He was said to have become attracted to her. Breaking a cast-iron rule, Berry went into the condemned cell on the night before the execution and sat with her for a time. He promised that he would not keep her alive a moment longer than necessary, although whether this grim prognostication gave her any comfort at all is not recorded. The following morning, 14 March 1887, barely two months after the murder, Berry accompanied his charge from the condemned cell to the gallows across an open courtyard. It had been snowing and the barely conscious Mrs Berry had great difficulty in walking the sixty yards to the execution shed. Berry said later that after the execution he cut off a lock of Mrs Berry's hair and kept it for luck over several years. However, he eventually decided that this grim memento actually brought him bad luck rather than good, and he destroyed it. Mrs Berry was the first criminal to be executed at Liverpool Prison (Walton Gaol).

2

A MYSTERIOUS STRANGER

Twenty-one miles north-west of Manchester is Blackburn (once known as Cotton Town), standing at the site where a Roman military road crossed the River Blakewater. Today, the main A674 runs through the middle of the town towards Accrington and Burnley, with Witton Country Park on its left at the eastern end, which debouches on to open moorland. The park's right-hand boundary is Buncer Lane, which is now to the left of its original position due to road improvements. But in 1892 the area, now occupied by a large modern housing estate, was much more open, with just a few rows of labourers' cottages.

On 8 November 1892 Alice, the nine-year-old daughter of farmer Edward Barnes of Redlam Farm, Witton, came running into the farmhouse at about noon, after spending the morning at Witton School. She was a big girl for her age and was already doing her share of work on the farm; today she knew that before she sat down at the kitchen table to eat her lunch she would have to take the cows into the park to graze, a journey of about 300 yards.

The way into the park was along Spring Lane, via a rickety footbridge over the River Blakewater, where there were two doors in the surrounding park wall, from which Buncer Lane then wound its way up a gradual hill. To the right of the main doors was a smaller wicket gate, which opened inwards. A sill, about 9in in height, lay at the foot of the wicket gate, which made it necessary for people to step over it when passing through. Alice, accompanied by her eight-year-old sister, Mary, collected the cows and drove them towards the park entrance. They were seen by twelve-year-old Elizabeth Riding, the daughter of Dr Thomas Riding, Head Keeper for General Fielden (a local notable), as she walked down Spring Lane on her way home.

Crossing the footbridge over the Blakewater, which at that stage was only a minor stream, and a few steps away from the park gates, she saw a man leaning against the railings close to the park doors. She was then distracted by the sight of the two little girls ushering the cattle into the park, and saw that the younger girl was turning back with one of the calves, although she could not see any reason for it.

Elizabeth now ran forward to give Alice Barnes some assistance, being well used to handling cattle in this then rural community. Having got the cows safely into the park, Elizabeth left Alice and turned for home, which was inside the park, stopping to talk to twelve-year-old Edith Duxbury for a few minutes. Edith had also seen the mysterious man standing by the railings and had not liked the look of him. Elizabeth agreed: 'That man doesn't look very promising,' she said. 'He stared at me so much that if I'd been by myself, I would have turned back.'

Edith and Elizabeth then went their separate ways. Elizabeth, going through the gates into the park and looking back the way she had come, saw that the mysterious man had disappeared.

Meanwhile, at Redlam Farm, Edward Barnes was looking at the clock on the mantelshelf. Alice had been gone for over half an hour now and Mary had returned with the calf fifteen minutes ago. 'She should have been back by now,' he muttered to himself. He shouted for his son and sent him off to the park to find his sister.

At twenty past one, Mrs Martha Hindle, a widow who lived in Whalley Old Road, Blackburn, walked along Spring Lane and across the footbridge into Buncer Lane. In front of her she saw the recumbent body of Alice Barnes lying face downwards just outside the big park doors, with her head towards the wicket gate. She bent down and touched the girl's leg – it felt cold – and quickly, she hurried into Buncer Lane to give the alarm.

Just a few minutes before, ten-year-old Harry Riding, Elizabeth's brother, had been on his way to school and running quickly towards the park doors, heading for Buncer Lane. As he approached, he saw a man leaning against the wall in a stooping position, just inside the doors. When the man saw Harry he jumped up and ran towards the wicket gate and went through. Harry saw that he had a child in his arms and heard a bump as the man let the child fall to the ground and ran over the footbridge. Frightened, the young boy ran off to the park lodge, where he found Mrs Ellen Ormerod, wife of the lodge keeper, who said later that she had seen the boy running towards her looking very frightened. Coming up to her, Harry gasped out that he had seen a man throw a boy over the wall (he had not been near enough to realise that it was, in fact, a girl). Mrs Ormerod told the boy that she would tell her husband as soon as he came in and Harry ran off again, out of the park. At the top of Spring Lane he met his friend Percy Thompson, who went back with him to the park doors and saw that the girl's body was now surrounded by a group of women, who collared the two lads and told them to fetch a policeman as quickly as possible. Just then they noticed Farmer Barnes approaching, having been told of the tragedy by his son, and watched as he knelt down and cradled the girl's head in his arms, his eyes wet with tears.

Another local farmer, Edward Southworth, then came up carrying a rug, which he placed tenderly over the girl's body, and stood with the others, awaiting the arrival of the police. The first policeman to appear was Constable Richard Ashworth,

A contemporary photograph of the murder site. (By kind permission of Cotton Town Digitisation Project)

The park lodge, where Harry Riding ran to tell what he had seen. (A. Hayhurst)

whose cottage in Selbourne Street, off Spring Lane, was only about thirty yards from the scene of the crime. He had just been settling down to his dinner when the two boys appeared and hammered urgently at his door. Muttering a curse under his breath, Ashworth went to see what all the fuss was about and was soon donning his uniform jacket and running towards the footbridge. Kneeling down, he felt the girl's body for a pulse, but could not find one. Examining the girl's face, he noticed something protruding from her mouth, which he thought was her tongue. Shouting to Farmer Southworth to fetch his shandry (a light cart on springs), the two men lifted the dead girl on to the cart and Southworth wheeled it off to the police station.

At about 2.30 p.m. Dr James Wheatley, the Police Surgeon and Medical Officer of Health for Blackburn, arrived at the Duckworth Street mortuary (which was soon seen to be a bizarre coincidence) to examine the body. He, like PC Ashworth, noticed something protruding from the dead girl's mouth and carefully tried to extract what he found to be a red handkerchief, which was covered in blood and which appeared to have been stuffed into the girl's mouth with considerable force. There was blood about the girl's lips and chin and a small cut on the forehead. The left hand was bloodstained and there was a considerable amount of earth in the right hand and in the nails. There were also other bruises about the body and the veins of the neck were distended. There was, however, no evidence that the girl had been violated. Cause of death, he opined, was due to suffocation from the handkerchief being crammed into her mouth. Alice Barnes was buried at St Leonard's church, Balderstone, on 12 November, when nearly 2,000 people lined the streets as the cortege went by.

The police had now started to search the area and became very interested in the print of a man's right boot, which had been found in the mud, close to where the body lay. The boot was heavily nailed on the sole in an unusual pattern, with eight nails on the outside of the sole being in a straight line, although the edge of the sole itself was curved. Local bootmaker, William Stirrup, told the police that he had never seen another boot nailed in that fashion. However, there was, at this stage, nothing to connect it to the murderer other than its presence at the scene of the crime.

Richard Wolstenholme, a Blackburn sub-postmaster, who also acted as police photographer, made a tracing of the footprint, which was then carefully compared to a plaster cast which had been taken. Another boot maker, Edward Mercer, agreed with Wolstenholme's findings and commented that the position of the nails might have been pricked out by machinery, but the nails had been put in by hand. His professional opinion was that the eight straight nails were just one individual's way of working.

Several people came forward in response to a police request, all claiming to have seen a man in the area of the murder scene at about noon, or shortly after. They included Elizabeth and Harry Riding, Edith Duxbury and James Smith, a shoemaker who was crossing the footbridge at five minutes to one and saw a man on the bridge leaning against the railings. Although the man had his back to him, he was sure that he was dark complexioned and was wearing a blue spotted muffler.

Alice Barnes' grave in St Leonard's Church, Balderstone.
(A. Hayhurst)

Detail from Alice Barnes' grave.
(A. Hayhurst)

Martha Southworth, thirteen years old, lived in Spring Lane and told the police that she was looking through her front window at about ten past one on the day of the murder, when she saw a man running past. Intrigued, she stood on the sofa to get a better look and saw the man turn the corner by Grimshaw's shop and go into Redlam, a local thoroughfare. John Walsh, a gas-meter inspector, also saw this man in Redlam and said that he took particular notice of the man's face. He also saw that the man's trousers were very dirty and he looked confused, although he did not think the man was drunk.

John William Riley, who lived in Broomfield Place, saw a man at about ten past one running up the street and making for a back passage into Vauxhall Street, from which he soon returned. Riley noticed that the man's trousers were badly mud-stained from the knees downwards. Mrs Emily O'Brien of Vauxhall Street told the police that she had seen a man pass her house carrying a muffler in his hand. He looked rather strange to her, but she thought that she knew him. The man went into the passage and put on his muffler, wiping his face with a handkerchief, then passed out of her view.

For the next couple of days, a total of six men were arrested on suspicion of being the mysterious stranger, but all were released without charge. A man named Tatlow, who had committed suicide by throwing himself in front of a train on the day after the murder, gave rise to much speculation, but was soon removed from police enquiries as his movements on the day of the murder were fully accounted for. The police were now at a loss. Several people had seen the mysterious man with the muffler, but no-one had so far named him. Then, on Sunday 13 November around 10 p.m., a group of policemen gathered quietly around the house of one Cross Duckworth, of 11 Primrose Terrace, Bower House Fold, Blackburn. Married, with a wife and two children, Duckworth was a labourer and an ex-soldier, having left the army on pension two years before. Amongst the policemen were Inspector William Dobson, Sergeant Richardson, PC Pomfret and Detective Superintendent Longstaffe. Dobson and Longstaffe went to the front door and the other two went round the back. The house was in darkness as the Inspector banged on the door, but a voice answered from inside and the door half opened, revealing a man partly dressed and holding a lighted candle.

'Are you Cross Duckworth?' asked Dobson.

'Yes,' replied the man.

'I suppose you know that we are police officers?' Dobson asked.

'I know now that you have told me,' said Duckworth. 'You have not come for me over that murder have you?'

'We have come to see if you will come with us to the police station,' the Inspector told him, 'as we want you to give an account of your whereabouts on Tuesday last.'

Duckworth nodded. 'I'll come,' he said, opening the door fully and admitting the policemen. They let Richardson and Pomfret in at the back door, then waited whilst Duckworth got dressed. He had almost finished when Dobson asked, 'Have you any other boots,' pointing to the pair Duckworth had on.

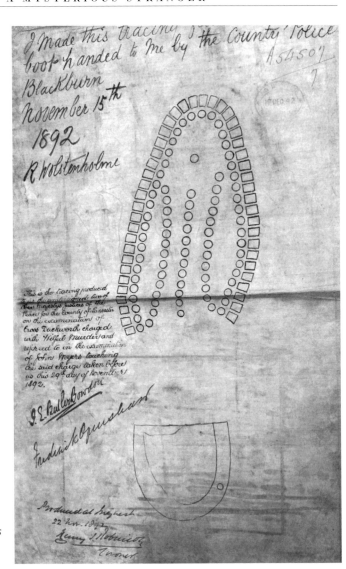

A drawing of the mysterious footprint found near the body. (National Archives)

'I've got another pair somewhere,' Duckworth said. 'You'll find them on the stairs in the back kitchen. I've not had them on since a week yesterday.'

Duckworth looked round for a muffler to put round his neck.

'Isn't that one there?' Dobson asked, pointing to a clothes peg on the wall.

'Yes, that's it. I have worn it all week,' replied Duckworth.

Examining it, Dobson saw that it appeared to have been recently laundered. PC Pomfret was now sent to find a cab and the party eventually arrived at the county police station at Blackburn. An hour later, Inspector Dobson and Sergeant Richardson went back to Duckworth's house and, after searching round, Richardson found a man's freshly laundered handkerchief in a kitchen drawer, which appeared to match the one found in the dead girl's mouth, and another sim-

Vauxhall Street, where Duckworth ran after the murder. (A. Hayhurst)

ilar one in a pile of dirty washing. He also took away a pair of men's boots, a rope with a running noose in it and a newspaper containing an account of the murder.

Duckworth was taken in front of Superintendent John Myers, who cautioned him and said, 'I am going to ask you to account for yourself on Tuesday the 8th last.'

The accused man then made a statement, in which he said that on that day he left his house at 7 a.m. and went straight to the Harrisons Arms and stayed there for half an hour. Then he went to the Corporation Inn at Bank Top and was there until half past eight, after which he went to the nearby Farmer's Arms and at 9.30 a.m., he was at the King Street railway sidings with his brother William, where he took a load of coal to Crook Street. At 12.30 p.m. he was in the Dun Horse Hotel and from there he went straight home. He insisted that he had then been at home all afternoon until 4 p.m. and the only people in the house had been him and his two children, aged six and ten. His wife worked in the local mill and did not come home for dinner. 'I generally shave clean,' he told the superintend-ent, 'but I had a few days growth that day.'

William Duckworth's statement backed up his brother's to a certain extent, but he said that after visiting several public houses with his brother and delivering the load of coal, he went back to the railway sidings. It would then have been quarter past twelve. He knew the Dun Horse, but had not been there in the last month, and he had never been in that inn with his brother.

The landlord of the Unicorn Inn at Bank Top, Robert Crook, said that he knew Cross Duckworth very well. He remembered him coming in about 11 a.m. on the 8th and he recalled him having three glasses of porter. He stayed till twenty min-utes to one and when he left, went straight into the vault of the Turner's Arms. His wife had shouted to Duckworth that he could share their meal of potato pie, but Duckworth turned the offer down, saying that he had to look after his children. The landlord saw him again later that day at 7 p.m., when Duckworth came in and read a report out loud from the *Northern Daily Telegraph*, concerning the death of Alice Barnes. According to the landlord Duckworth said, 'It's a bonny shame, whoever has done it,' and then commented that he had heard that the police had picked up a tramp. Crook noticed that Duckworth had on a new pair of ribbed trousers and remarked on them, but the man made no reply.

Once news of Cross Duckworth's arrest became known, other people came forward with tales of having seen him in the vicinity of the crime. Spinster, Mary Davies, walking up Griffin Street going towards Redlam, had seen him and it looked to her as if he was drunk (she might well have been right considering the amount of time he had spent in public houses that morning). It was then about quarter to one. Richard Porter said that he had met Duckworth on the 8th, walking in the direction of Spring Lane and noticed that the man had been drinking. It would be about a three or four minutes' walk to get to the footbridge by the murder scene and it was then a few minutes to one.

Duckworth was taken in front of Blackburn magistrates on Monday 14 November, and in reply to a charge of murder he said, 'I cannot see why I am charged with murder, because I cannot see that there is any proof that it is me that committed the crime. I am innocent of the charge, I can assure you.'

Despite his protestations, Duckworth was committed to the Liverpool Winter Assizes, where he stood trial for his life. The judge, Mr Justice Grantham, had set aside a special day for the trial, which would start, he announced, at 10 a.m. sharp. When that time arrived, the only people in court were the jurors and a large number of reporters and, despite the judge's strictures, it was not until 10.30 a.m. that the judge himself and the High Sheriff arrived and took their places. Duckworth entered the dock, looking composed, and in answer to the charge said 'Not Guilty' in a low voice. Whether he was suffering from any kind of ill health is not known, but his counsel, Mr McKeand, asked the judge if his client could sit down in the dock and the judge agreed.

The details of the case were described by the prosecutor, Dr O'Feeley, and the jury were provided with a large plan of the ground involved. 'There was no doubt,' said O'Feeley, 'that when the girl took the cows into the park, a man was standing on the footbridge only a few yards from her and the jury would have no doubt, when they hear the evidence, that the man, whoever he was, was the murderer of the child.' In fact, there was little or no evidence that the mysterious stranger on the bridge had murdered anybody. Although it might be possible to place Cross Duckworth near the scene of the crime, the evidence that he had actually harmed Alice Barnes was far from watertight.

O'Feeley proposed to call about forty witnesses, some of whom would trace Duckworth's movements early on the morning of 8 November up till the time that a man was seen on the bridge. Another group of witnesses would identify the prisoner as that man and there would then be evidence of his progress, from street to street, as he fled from the scene, and at some places where he appeared to be hastening away from the scene of the crime. Having traced the man's progress past Southworth's house, across the road into Vauxhall Street, the counsel asked why any man should take that curious circuit through narrow lanes and back yards, unless it was to avoid identification from people he might meet on the road. He then pointed out to the jury that when the police visited the prisoner, the first words the accused had said to them were, 'Have you come for me about this murder?' Yet no mention of the murder had been made at that stage.

Counsel went on, 'When Duckworth was asked to account for his movements on the morning of the murder, he told the police that he was with his brother and the brother confirmed this, but had recently altered his statement and now said that the accused was never with him at all on the day of the murder, but on the Thursday following. The evidence of the brother and of accused's own daughter would prove that the prisoner's voluntary statement to the police was untrue from start to finish.'

He then dealt with the evidence of the handkerchiefs and the boot, telling the jury that there could be little doubt that the owner of the boot, which made the imprint, was the same man who had thrust the handkerchief down Alice Barnes' throat. What effect this atrocious farrago of misstatements had on the jury, we shall never know, but O'Feeley must have known that his bald statement that the boot print could be traced to the murderer was complete conjecture and should have had no place in an English court of law, let alone being put forward by the prosecution. Mr Justice Grantham, however, did not see fit to intervene and neither, unfortunately for Cross Duckworth, did his own counsel, who must surely have been nodding off at that moment.

Mrs Hindle, PC Ashworth and Farmer Southworth all described how they found the body, then the landlord of the Unicorn said that Duckworth had been in his bar until twenty minutes to one and then again in the evening. He had read the item in the *Northern Daily Telegraph* in a normal voice, with no sign of nervousness. Richard Porter estimated that he saw Duckworth in Redlam about ten minutes to one. He would then be about three to four minutes' walk from the bottom of Buncer Lane. Henry Barker, a shopkeeper on Redlam, saw the accused pass his shop at six minutes to one, when he would be about 150 yards from the footbridge. (Quite how all these witnesses were able to be so dogmatic, with times given to the minute, is one of the minor mysteries of this case.)

Barker then told how he had been taken to the police office and had there been asked to have a look at a man in the next room. 'I did not see him properly,' he said, but admitted that he had identified the man as the one he had seen passing his shop. At this point the court adjourned for lunch and when it resumed, it was seen that General Fielden MP and his wife, with Mr Coddington, the local MP, had been given seats in the grand jury box.

Twelve-year-old Edith Duxbury now gave her evidence, after which O'Feeley pointed to the dock and asked her, 'Was that the man you saw on the bridge?'

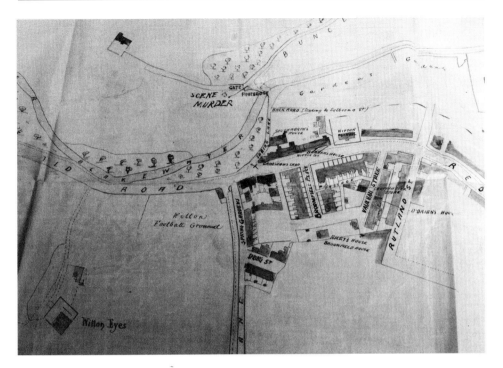

Plan of the murder site at Witton. (National Archives)

'Yes,' replied the young girl, who must have been somewhat intimidated by the bewigged judge and counsel as she stood in the witness box. Elizabeth Riding was next and told the court that she had been taken to see several men, but none of them resembled the man, except the prisoner. She had not been sure when she picked him out at first, but she said, 'I am sure now.'

Henry Broad said that he had seen the girls talking together near the gates and noticed a man on the bridge at five minutes to one. At quarter past one, the man walked past him again and he had identified the prisoner from his general appearance. When asked if he saw the man's face at all he replied, 'I don't remember his face. I remember his clothes.'

'Were you quite sure of this when you saw him at the police station?'

'I was quite sure when I got close to him,' Broad replied.

Young Harry Riding also identified the accused, but also admitted that when he had first seen him the man had had his back turned to him, and after dropping the girl had run off. 'They often talked about the matter at home,' the ten-year-old boy said.

Superintendent Myers produced the handkerchief and the plaster cast of the boot. The cast was handed up to the judge and those present noticed, with interest, that he moved a square of black material from a side-table to his desk, to make room for it. Myers told the jury, 'At no time did any of the witnesses identify any person other than Duckworth.' The court then adjourned for the day – obviously Mr Justice Grantham had underestimated how long the trial was going to last.

Next day, Richard Wolstenholme, the man who had done the tracing of the boot sole, said that there were some discrepancies between the casting and his tracing, but said that they could be accounted for by shrinking of the plaster on drying.

The handkerchief was then dealt with and Thomas Birtwistle JP, Her Majesty's Inspector of Factories, with forty-seven years of experience in the trade, said that he was of the opinion that all three handkerchiefs were of the same counts in weft and twist: 'They were all manufactured at the same time and were part of the same order,' he said. The dirty handkerchief found at the prisoner's house was most like the one crammed into the girl's mouth. Cross-examined by Mr McKeand, he had to admit that a very large number of similar handkerchiefs had been sold and that there were differences in all of them. This prompted the judge to suggest that the handkerchief evidence be withdrawn. 'A miss is as good as a mile,' he said, 'there are only slight differences, but they are enough.' The handkerchiefs were withdrawn, but the damage had been done. The jury must have struggled to keep them from interfering with their judgement when it came time for the verdict.

For the defence, William Duckworth said that his brother had been with him all Tuesday morning. A little peeved, Dr O'Feeley snapped, 'Are you sure it was not the Thursday?'

'Yes,' replied William.

'Just look at your statement before the coroner,' said the prosecutor. 'Do you still persist in saying that you saw him on the Tuesday?'

'Yes,' he replied.

Next witness was the accused man's own daughter, ten-year-old Margaret Ann, who said that she remembered the day the little girl was killed and that she and her sister were at school that morning and she prepared their dinner, before going back to school at twenty minutes to two. There was no one at home apart from her and her sister and she left a bowl of food on the table. When she came back at half past four, the food had gone. She never saw her father all that day.

In reply to Mr McKeand, the young girl said that she did not know today's date, nor could she tell the time by the court clock. (This is another instance of precise timing being open to serious doubt in this case.) She had been taken into the back room to be questioned by the police, she said, and she had been very frightened.

Mr McKeand then outlined the case for the defence and said that in the first instance, it would be one of alibi. He would call five young men who would say that when the one o'clock gun went off, the accused was 1,200 yards away from the foot-bridge at Duckworth Street. He would present other evidence to show that a terrible mistake had been made in this case and there was sufficient doubt about it to prevent the jury, as fair-minded men, from sending the accused to the scaffold.

It then turned out that the judge had himself walked over the ground where the murder took place and the general country surrounding it. Several times he interrupted and intimated that he knew exactly what the witnesses were talking about when they described the area: 'I thought it safer to go over the ground myself, as so much depended on the evidence of children,' he told the court.

The 'five young men' were then called to say that Duckworth was with them at around the time of the murder and all agreed that Duckworth was drunk. The judge seemed annoyed with one witness, Robert Wilson: 'Drunk! Drunk! Drunk!' he exclaimed. 'You ought to be ashamed of yourselves.' The court then adjourned for lunch, and on resuming Dr O'Feeley said that he would not seek to rely on the evidence of the boot print and/or the tracing, as it would not be safe.

Mr McKeand then continued. 'My unfortunate client has been tried in every public house in Lancashire, but I implore the jury not to pay any attention to those who clamour for this man's blood. An innocent little girl has been cruelly butchered, but the vital question,' he said, 'is whether the prisoner was the man that did it. The jury ought to view with the greatest of care and circumspection the evidence of children, and especially girls just blooming into womanhood, when the imagination is so fertile and when the slightest suggestion made by an older person might be easily believed.' He continued in a tremulous voice: 'With the boots and the handkerchiefs, two threads of evidence in the case were absolutely scattered to the winds and as to the other evidence against my client, I cannot remember another case when witnesses have come forward in a life and death case and given their evidence with such recklessness! Fortunately for the interests of justice,' he told the jury, 'there is in Blackburn a time-gun, which enables witnesses to say with accuracy what time they saw the accused, drunk, in Duckworth Street.'

Mr McKeand then attacked other prosecution witnesses with ferocity: 'Martha Southworth's evidence was absolutely stuff and nonsense and utterly worthless for the purpose of identification,' he said. He suggested that all the witnesses who had placed Cross Duckworth at the scene were mistaken and that the man they saw was so great a stranger to the locality as not to know his way through the back streets. The accused man's evidence had been corroborated by the witnesses he had called, which made it absolutely impossible for the prisoner to have been the murderer.

'Finally,' he told the jury, 'the spirit of that little girl is crying aloud for vengeance. Throughout the length and breadth of this great country, there has been a terrible cry for the blood of that man. But I ask you not to be led away by that cry, but to deliberate, for it is far better that this crime should go unpunished than that the bright, shining altar of justice should be stained with innocent blood.'

Doctor O'Feeley replied for the prosecution, saying that the alibi rested on the evidence of Wilson, who had told his four companions that the drunken man they saw was Duckworth. On the other hand, eleven witnesses swore to Duckworth being on the way to the scene of the crime. The judge said that all the evidence pointed to the murderer attacking the child for the purpose of violation, and he either went down the lane with the object of meeting a girl or was suddenly tempted.

'It was right,' he told the jury, 'for me to tell you that although on matters of fact children are reliable witnesses, yet in dealing with impressions they are not so reliable as adults.' All the evidence of the prisoner being on the bridge and in Spring Lane is that of children and it should not be lost sight of that all, at one time or another, had said they were not sure about him. It would not be safe to rely entirely on the evidence of the children, although the evidence of the adults has served to strengthen the case against the accused.'

The jury departed at 5.30 p.m. and returned at half past six with a verdict of 'Guilty', but with a recommendation to mercy. Donning the black cap, the judge then pronounced the sentence of death: 'The jury have recommended him to mercy,' he said, 'and I will forward that recommendation to the proper place.'

'Thank you, my lord,' Duckworth replied and was then taken down. The judge then asked the jury on what grounds they were making their recommendation, and the foreman of the jurors said it was because he had not deliberately and intentionally murdered the child, but that death followed upon his attempt to stifle her cries during his assault upon her.

An appeal failed, despite the secretaries of various Blackburn trade unions writing to the Home Secretary to ask for the Royal Prerogative to be exercised, saying that they had followed the case closely from the beginning and were strongly of the opinion that the prosecution evidence was altogether too weak to warrant a man's life being forfeited. Representing 30,000 hands in the town of Blackburn, they wrote: 'It is the feeling of almost all of our members that the prisoner should not be hung on the evidence given at the trial.'

They received only the usual formal letter from the Home Secretary, informing that regrettably he could not see any reason to interfere with the process of the law. On the day before the execution, Duckworth was allowed to see his wife and children for the last time. The youngest child suddenly blurted out, 'Dada, aren't you coming home tonight?' which reduced everyone, including the warders, to tears.

On 3 January 1893, at 8 a.m., Cross Duckworth was executed at Walton Gaol, Liverpool. The High Sheriff had decided not to admit representatives of the press, as was usual at that time, and the execution was witnessed only by Mr Haverfield, the Prison Governor, the Reverend David Morris, prison chaplain, and prison officials.

From the time that James Billington entered the cell, to the condemned man falling through the trap, was less than five minutes, more than many later executions, but Billington had no assistant. Cross Duckworth had spent a disturbed night, which now showed on his face. According to one account he had 'an unutterably weary appearance' as he breakfasted, having received the ministrations of the Reverend Morris.

At half past seven, Duckworth had been moved from the hospital wing to the condemned cell, weeping bitterly and appearing very shaky. Once the pinioning had been completed the Reverend Morris, in a flowing surplice and purple stole, led the procession, which went from the condemned cell to a courtyard, over which it was necessary to pass to reach the execution shed. Snow was falling heavily and Duckworth was soon covered in flakes. Deathly pale and with teeth chattering, the condemned man walked in a daze and, seemingly unaware of his surroundings, allowed himself to be positioned on the trap by Billington. According to the *Daily Post* he protested his innocence to the last. A small group of spectators had huddled together outside the prison, seeking shelter from the snowstorm and the biting north-east wind, and after reading the official notice of execution they had hurried away out of the cold.

Telegram confirming Duckworth's execution. (National Archives)

In the files of the National Archives there is a letter from the Reverend David Morris to the Home Secretary, stating that Duckworth confessed to him that he was guilty of the murder on the morning of the execution. 'I did commit this crime,' Duckworth had told him, 'But God knows I had no thoughts in my heart to murder the little lamb.'

Note: The *Daily Telegraph* of Saturday, 3 February 1934 carried an article headed 'Roman Church and an Asquith Story'. It concerned an article published by Lady Violet Bonham Carter in the October *Strand Magazine*, in which she said that her father, when Home Secretary, suffered from misgivings over having refused a reprieve in the case of a man sentenced to be hanged for child murder. She went on to say that after the execution, her father was intensely relieved by a letter confirming that the man had confessed to his guilt. This letter, she wrote, came from a Roman Catholic priest. (The text given differed in almost every detail from the actual letter written by David Morris, who was in fact a Church of England clergyman, having officiated at the prison for twenty years.) The Roman Catholic newspaper *The Tablet* was horrified at this alleged disclosure and protested in print that no Roman Catholic priest would ever break the seal of the confessional. Lady Bonham Carter stuck to her guns and insisted that her father would never have made a mistake upon such a matter. The files at the National Archives would seem to say otherwise.

3

THE HORROR UPSTAIRS

Liverpool, 1893

Number 4 Gildart Street, Liverpool, was an ordinary three-storey house on the corner of Bayhorse Lane. The ground floor was fitted out as a shop, with shelves and a counter, and there was living accommodation on two floors above. There lived Mrs Margaret Walber and her husband of five years, fifty-five-year-old John, who brought in a spasmodic income as a French polisher. Both had been married before and this second try at marital bliss was not a happy one.

Mrs Walber, two years younger than her husband, was often heard berating him for frequenting a brothel run by one Anne Connolly in nearby Oake Street, something that John Walber always stoutly denied. However, John had in fact known Miss Connolly for about thirty years, and, seventeen years ago, they had lived together for a short time, although Miss Connolly always said that as soon as she discovered that he was married she threw him out. Since then, according to Miss Connolly, she had seen neither hide nor hair of him. Whether this story was true is doubtful, seeing that Oake Street was only a few yards from the Walber's home and his wife's suspicions had resulted in John sleeping in the top room at Gildart Street, formerly the marital bedroom, whilst his wife moved her bed downstairs to the shop, where she now usually slept.

On 2 May 1893, John Walber called at the house in Oake Street; he had hardly been sat down for two or three minutes when his wife burst in, asking if her husband was there.

'You can come and take him,' said Anne Connolly, 'he's not wanted here.'

Plainly beside herself, Margaret Walber grabbed her husband, who, despite being a fairly heavy man and well built, was knocked to the floor. Feeling in his pockets, she took out what money he had and then kicked him as he lay there. Walber made no attempt to stop the assault and his wife then said, 'Stop there. I don't want you,' after which she flounced out.

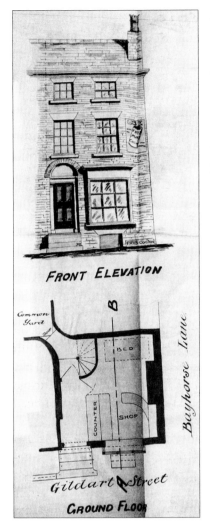

FRONT ELEVATION

GROUND FLOOR

Elevation and plan of the Gildart Street premises.
(National Archives)

From time to time John Murray, Margaret Walber's son from her first marriage, came home and shared the top room with his stepfather – an arrangement that did not appear to cause any trouble. The lad was of Irish extraction and worked as a street musician. For the past two years he had been in Ireland, but he had been staying at Gildart Street since June that year. In early November he had heard his mother and stepfather arguing about something, but said that they were always 'arguing and plaguing each other' and thought nothing of it.

The middle floor of the cramped little house was rented to Mary Vause, who had been there for about four months and who shared the room with her boyfriend, James Bairstow Pearson, a labourer. During the time they lived there, Mary Vause said that she often heard the Walbers arguing, and James Pearson said that in November 1893 he had heard yet another row between John Walber and his wife, with her shouting at him that she would not have him going to Anne Connolly's house again. This time John Murray had intervened, saying, 'That's enough, mother, that'll do,' and his stepfather then said, 'No, No, Maggie, I won't go there again.'

What neither James Pearson nor John Murray appeared to have noticed, or if they did they took care not to comment on it, was that for the past few months John Walber had been a virtual prisoner in the top floor room, his wife having fitted a stout chain to the outside of the door, which she inserted into a hasp and locked with a padlock. Mary Vause was aware that Mrs Walber took food up to her husband from time to time, during which she often heard cries of 'Murder!' and 'Oh!' from John Walber, although she never seems to have enquired from her landlady what was going on.

On Sunday 12 November, she saw Mrs Walber go up to the top room and later heard John Murray saying to her, 'Don't, mother, that's enough!' On another occasion, Mrs Walber had said to Mary that she would keep her husband locked up until she had to carry him out in a box, and several times Mary had heard Margaret shouting at her husband that he would never leave the room alive.

On 13 November, Elizabeth Walber, John's sister, paid a visit to 4 Gildart Street and asked to see her brother. Margaret Walber was in the shop at the time and said to her, 'Your brother is upstairs and I intend to keep him there,' at which Elizabeth demanded to see her brother immediately. The two women climbed the stairs to the top room, where Elizabeth saw that the door was chained. Without a word, Mrs Walber unlocked the chain and allowed her to enter the room, to find John Walber in bed, completely naked apart from a woollen shirt. Elizabeth looked round, but none of his other clothes seemed to be in the room.

'John,' his sister said, 'What are you doing here?'

He made no reply, although she could see that he was awake. To her, he looked strange and bewildered and the thought flashed through her mind that he might be in a drugged stupor.

'Would you like me to get you a doctor, or a clergyman, John?' she asked the recumbent figure.

'You shall fetch no-one here to him,' said his wife sharply. 'One week he pretends to be blind and another week he pretends to be paralysed, it's all mockery,' she said, motioning Elizabeth to leave the room. Mrs Walber carefully chained the door up again and the two went back downstairs. Whatever the conversation that then took place between the two women, Elizabeth Walber stayed the night and left at nine o'clock the following morning without attempting to see her brother again. The next time that she saw him, he was dead.

Around the same time, Mrs Nancy Hannah was visiting Mary Vause when she heard a cry from the room upstairs. 'Hello,' a voice shouted, followed by knocking on the floor. Mrs Hannah shouted down the stairs to Mrs Walber, who was in the shop. 'Your husband's shouting,' she called, to which Margaret replied, 'Let the old bugger wait until I am ready.'

Ten minutes later, Margaret Walber went upstairs and Mrs Hannah and Mary heard angry words and sounds of scuffling. 'Murder!' shouted John Walber, a word that was often used in the house but to which, inexplicably, no one seemed to react. Just as she was leaving, Mrs Hannah saw Margaret Walber and asked what was going on upstairs. 'Oh, he's just acting again,' said Margaret and bade her goodbye.

On Thursday 16 November, about noon, Mrs Walber sent out for some whisky, which she shared with her son John, Mary Vause and James Pearson. In the course of conversation, Mrs Walber said that she had flypaper in the shop which she would not mind giving to her husband.[*] John Murray put down his glass of whisky. 'Don't do that to the poor old man,' he said and lapsed back into silence.

Shortly afterwards, Mrs Walber announced that she was going to the post office in nearby Pembroke Place, on an errand, and invited Mary Vause to go with her.

---

[*] Flypapers could be bought at any chemist's shop and consisted of a six-inch square of paper, impregnated with arsenic. The method of use was to place the flypaper on a plate and pour boiling water on it. This released the arsenic; flies landed on the liquid and drank it and expired from arsenical poisoning. However, it was well known that a couple of fly papers could supply enough arsenic liquor to kill a human being, despite which the papers continued on open sale until well into the 1930s.

There, Mrs Walber drew out the sum of £4, and on the way back home the two women called at a public house on Bayhorse Lane, where they saw Mrs Ellen Mottram, who was living apart from her husband in a flat at 14 Gildart Street. Mrs Mottram had known Mrs Walber for about three years and patronised her shop. She too had often heard Margaret Walber upbraiding her husband and noticed that, on this particular day, Mrs Walber seemed strangely excited. Beckoning John Sullivan, a labourer, over to them, Mrs Walber bought drinks for all four, and then blurted out that she would give a sovereign to anyone who would smash Anne Connolly's windows and then give Miss Connolly a good hiding. She also said that she would mutilate her husband right up to the navel before any other woman should enjoy him. Mrs Mottram finished her drink and left, no doubt pondering what she had just heard. Turning to Sullivan Margaret said, 'What do you think? My husband has taken tea and sugar and other bits and pieces to Anne Connolly and I'll give her summat, and him as well.' Sullivan followed Mrs Mottram's example, drank up and left.

Later, Margaret Walber arrived home and saw her son John there. In John's opinion his mother was 'too boozed altogether', although this did not stop her from twice demanding a glass of ale, which John Murray obligingly fetched for her. A short while afterwards she went upstairs to the top floor and John followed her, finding his stepfather sitting on the floor by his bed. The tweed trousers he had on belonged to John, but making no remark about this he turned round and went back downstairs into the cellar. Whilst he was there, he heard a noise, which he thought at first was in the street. Deciding to go back to his stepfather's room, he found to his horror that Walber was sitting on the floor with his back to a packing case and his head bent forward to the right side of his chest. The head and face were soaked with much blood and the room was in great disorder, with blood on the floor, walls and bedclothes. Hardly knowing what he was doing, John Murray picked up his fiddle, which had been propped up against the wall and took it down to the cellar, where he hid it in a corner. Leaving the house as quickly as he could, he went to Garston and slept that night in a common lodging house, going the next day to Dublin. It is one of the enduring mysteries of this case how so many people could have seen and heard Margaret Walber's atrocious treatment of her husband, but yet made no attempt to let the authorities know about it.

Finally, at about 10.30 a.m. on 17 November, PC 135 Richard James was called to the house by James Pearson. The policeman saw Mrs Walber in the shop and exchanged a few words with her, then went upstairs and found the body of John Walber in the top room. The body was quite cold and was clothed in a shirt, trousers, vest and socks. What little furniture there was in the room was in disorder and there were broken dishes and part of a broken lamp globe on the floor. Also on the floor was a bunch of hair, which appeared to have been cut from the right side of the dead man's beard.

About 3.45 p.m. the house was visited by Dr Joseph Stanley Kellett Smith, who carefully examined the body and then made little sketches of the room. Next day, he conducted a post-mortem, which disclosed a large cut on the left forearm of the deceased and several clean cuts to the face, all of which appeared to have been made with a knife. There were three slightly jagged cuts to the right cheek and a contused wound with dirt in the depth of it over each eyebrow, which the doctor thought had been caused by kicks. The genitals were bruised and wounded, as though by a kick. Some of the cuts to the face and head were dangerous and could have been caused by the broken lamp globe, which had been found in the room. Cause of death was given as shock and loss of blood.

'None of the wounds,' said Dr Smith, 'could have been self-inflicted.' A broken chamber pot, which had bloodstains on it, was found on a lamp pedestal and taken away for examination.

Detective Inspector Andrew Bryson, who had also been summoned to the crime scene, noted that there were bloodstains from a pool of blood on the floor to where the body was propped up against the packing case. It looked as though the body had been dragged across the floor to where it had been found. In addition, blood splashes reached half way up the walls. He also noted the chain that had been used to secure the door from the outside and later, he took away with him a pair of Mrs Walber's stays which had blood on them, as had the skirt which she had been wearing, and her boots. Margaret Walber was detained in the detective office and was interviewed on the following morning, when she asked the policeman what she was being kept for.

'For causing the death of your husband,' she was told, and she then replied, 'I will tell you all I know about it.' Having made a statement, she told the Inspector, 'I was very drunk and did not know what I was doing.' The statement, written by Detective Sergeant John Ramage, as the prisoner could not write, read as follows:

> I lived with my husband at 4 Gildart Street. On Thursday afternoon, my son came downstairs and told me that my husband had John's trousers on and was lying on the floor. I went up and he was lying on the floor and he would not speak to me. I took the chain off the door. I thought he was shamming and struck him across the head with the door chain. I came downstairs then. My husband has been going to a brothel in Oake Street kept by Annie Connolly and he robbed my shop, taking tobacco and tea to her. I took him back and he always pretended to be ill and wanted to get out and I had to chain him into the bedroom and take his clothes from him and put them in the cellar. When my son told me his father was up and had his trousers on, I was angry and thought he was only acting again to get out. When I struck him across the head with the chain, he never spoke. I was drunk at the time and don't remember what more I did to him. Mrs Pearson [Mary Vause] called me downstairs and said my son had gone. I went down and I missed £4 from my purse. I have not seen my son since. When I got up next morning, I never thought of what I had done to my husband but looked for my son and saw my husband lying on the floor. I told my clergyman that I was keeping my husband in and he said, 'You are doing quite right.'

St George's Hall, Liverpool, the scene of Margaret Walber's trial. (Author's collection)

Liverpool Prison (Walton Gaol) as it is today. (A. Hayhurst)

Modern-day site of 4 Gildart Street. (A. Hayhurst)

The statement bore Mrs Walber's cross, witnessed by Inspector Bryson and Sergeant Ramage.

An inquest was held on the dead man, which was adjourned until Monday 27 November and again until 4 December. Elizabeth Walber described how she had visited her brother, and in a written statement said that she had asked to see him and was told by Mrs Walber, 'He is upstairs. I have chained him there.' When asked 'Why?' Mrs Walber had replied, 'To keep him from bad company, as he is in the habit of going with bad people.' Elizabeth then went up and saw her brother, and formed the opinion that he was sober. Then she told how she passed the night sitting in a chair in the shop, whilst Mrs Walber slept on the sofa. Next morning, she left without seeing her brother again but gave no reason why. From the time she arrived, just before noon on the Monday, till her leaving time, just after nine on Tuesday morning, she saw no food taken up to her brother (nor, apparently, did she express a wish to take some up herself).

Elizabeth told the inquest that Mr Walber had been in America for some years and had got married there, but had deserted his wife and come back to England. Five years ago, he had married his current wife. (It is not certain whether John Walber ever took the trouble to divorce his first wife, who was said now to be living in Boston, Massachusetts, and thus whether his marriage to Margaret was legal.) Both the Walbers were of 'drinking habits' said Elizabeth, but seemed happy enough together.

Mary Vause gave evidence of the constant rowing between Walber and his wife; she blamed him for going with Annie Connolly. All the time Mary was living at the

Extract from the Huddersfield Daily Chronicle, *3 April 1894. (Author's collection)*

THE EXTRAORDINARY MURDER IN LIVERPOOL.

EXECUTION OF A WOMAN.

Margaret Walber, aged 53, was executed at Walton Gaol, on Monday morning, for the murder of her husband, John Walber (55), under circumstances so cruel and atrocious as to call for the remark from the judge that it was surprising that what she did was possible in the heart of Liverpool. Walber was her second husband. They had been married about five years, and they led an unhappy life, both of them being addicted to drink. The husband had formed a connection with a woman named Conolly, and while he was visiting this woman Margaret Walber came in and attacked him. She then confined him in a garret, which she chained and padlocked, and where she used to abuse him. Here he was found dead on November 16th, the room being like a shambles. He had evidently been beaten over the head with a chain or earthenware utensil and a lamp, both of which were smashed, the place being smeared all over with blood. The woman admitted striking him over the head with a chain.

No effort had been made to obtain a commutation of the sentence, and the wretched woman only had one visitor, her son, to whom she admitted the justice of the sentence. The last sacraments of the Church were administered to her on Sunday. Reporters were not admitted to the gaol. A crowd began to assemble at an early hour outside the gaol, where a thick fog prevailed, rendering it impossible to see the black flag a few yards away. A bell began to toll a few minutes before eight, and at eight precisely the black flag was hoisted, and the crowd began to disperse. The woman was attended by the Roman Catholic chaplain, to whom she expressed deep penitence for her crime.

Soon after the hoisting of the black flag reporters were informed that the Governor of the gaol was too busy to see them, but that the execution had been performed, and that the woman was dead. The doctor said the executioner could not have done his work more expeditiously. No information was forthcoming as to the last hours of the condemned. Billington, the executioner, was accompanied by his assistant, Thompson.

shop, she thought Mr Walber had been chained upstairs and had not been in any employment. She had also heard Margaret Walber tell her husband that he would never leave the upstairs room alive. On the day of the murder, she heard Margaret tell her son about the flypapers and heard him begging her not to do it. Mrs Walber had also said to her on the 16th that she had 'done five' (meaning years in prison) and would do another ten for her husband. By mid-afternoon, when Margaret discovered that her son had gone and had taken her £4 with him, she was definitely drunk. On the morning of the 17th she had come into Mary Vause's room and said, 'My son has killed John. John is dead,' after which James Pearson called the police.

Ellen Mottram, Nancy Hannah, Ann Connolly and John Sullivan also told their stories. Police evidence and that of the two doctors followed. The court was told that John Murray had been arrested in Ireland and was being brought to Liverpool to be charged with the murder of John Walber, but he was later released.

The coroner's jury found Margaret Walber guilty of the murder of her husband. She was tried at Liverpool Assizes before Mr Justice Day, where she was found guilty and sentenced to death. Executioner James Billington and a mysterious 'assistant' named Thompson (but who might have been someone from Billington's family), ensured that Margaret Walber paid the penalty ordained by law on 2 April 1893.

The Walber file at the National Archives was, for 116 years, catalogued under the name 'Walker' and so anyone searching for it would have been unsuccessful. Enquiries were instituted by the author and the discovery was made that the name on the file had been misread, with a 'k' substituted for the 'b'. Thus, the public have access to the file for the first time, which is now available under the correct name.

Gildart Street and Bayhorse Lane are now unrecognisable, having been rebuilt, although the exact site of the shop can still be ascertained.

4

THE HANGMAN PASSING BY

Bolton, 1901

James Billington had had a distinguished career in the post of hangman, officiating at his first execution on 26 August 1884, when Joseph Laycock paid the supreme penalty for murdering his wife and their four children. Being hangman was not, of course, sufficiently well paid to be a full-time occupation and Billington, as well as all the other hangmen in modern times, had perforce to obtain a more permanent job to keep body and soul together. Like many others of his craft, he chose that of publican, after all, it was the ideal job; when called upon, he could slip away for a couple of days, leaving his wife to run the business, and in no time he would be back behind the bar, dispensing good cheer and pints of ale.

In 1901, he was landlord of the Derby Arms Hotel in Churchgate, Bolton and his sons, William and John, both of whom had joined the other family 'business', lived nearby, working as barbers. One of James' regular customers was a man called Patrick McKenna, who lived at 5 Kestor Street, Bolton, with his wife Anna. McKenna was a joiner by trade, but times were hard and he had found it difficult to get work. Currently, he was working as a labourer, which he felt was insulting to him – this did nothing to soften his temper.

For this reason, they had taken in lodgers to their little terraced home, a Mr and Mrs Palmer, but whilst this did ease the financial position somewhat, the house was small and cramped, and Anna McKenna soon noticed that the Palmers were getting on Patrick's nerves, as a result of which he was drinking more than usual and was spending a lot of his free time in the Derby Arms. Despite their precarious finances, Patrick frequently took days off work, which he spent drinking, and there were regular rows with his wife about money. He also accused her of being a little too friendly with Mr Palmer, a suggestion that she hotly rejected.

On Monday, 30 September 1901, Patrick McKenna had another of his days off, which, as usual, he spent drinking, and around noon he appeared at 17 Kestor

James Billington. (Author's collection)

Street, the home of his son John and his wife
Emma. Anna McKenna was with them when
Patrick arrived and there then began a spat
between Patrick and his wife. In common with
many workers, the McKennas had a working
relationship with the local pawnbroker; often
the only means of them surviving until payday,
and Anna had just returned from one of her
regular visits.

'I suppose you've been to the pawnshop?'
Patrick said roughly. Anna looked at him and
said nothing. 'Give me tuppence,' McKenna
grunted. Anna stared at him. 'I'll give you
nothing,' she snapped. The look on McKenna's
face hardened. 'Then I'll damned well cut your bloody head off before the day's
out with my razor,' he snarled and left the house, still cursing to himself.

Emma McKenna went over to the door and bolted it after him. This was the right
thing for her to do, for within ten minutes Patrick McKenna was back, hammer-
ing on the front door and doing his best to break it open. The feisty Emma opened
the door and pushed her father-in-law away. McKenna, obviously drunk, fell over
onto the pavement, but recovered and clambered to his feet, trying to get hold of
Emma, who shoved him down again. Seeing there was no immediate chance of forc-
ing an entrance, Patrick staggered off down the street. Anna McKenna, who had
been much affected by the happenings of the past half hour, was unwilling to return
to her own home, so Emma suggested that she should rest awhile upstairs in their
house until things quietened down. For the rest of the afternoon things were quiet,
although Emma kept the bolt drawn on the door in case McKenna made another
appearance.

Around five o'clock, Emma's next-door neighbour, Mrs Elizabeth Fay, came in and
shortly afterwards Patrick McKenna appeared again, still angry. 'Have you seen my
old woman?' he asked Elizabeth roughly.

'No,' was the short answer, at which McKenna replied, 'Perhaps she'll be in bed
with Palmer,' and when Mrs Fay made no reply he continued, 'I'll go and see for
myself,' and turning on his heel he went in the direction of No. 5. Soon afterwards
Mrs Fay went back to her own house, and twenty minutes later she heard a scream
from No. 17. It sounded like Emma's voice and seconds later the woman came running into No. 19 and begged Elizabeth to come back to her house. 'He has cut the old
woman's throat with a razor,' she sobbed.

Doing as she was asked, Elizabeth hurried to No. 17 and looking through the
open front door, which led straight into the front room, saw Anna McKenna sitting in a chair near the door, blood pouring from her throat. She was not yet dead

The Derby Arms Hotel (on the right), Bolton, where hangman James Billington was the licensee. (Courtesy of Bolton Local Archives)

and had enough strength to lift her hand and motion for Elizabeth to go away, which she did, running off down the street to the police station.

It so happened that at that time, William Billington, James's son, was returning from a football match, a local derby between Bolton Wanderers and Bury. Walking along Kestor Street he saw a crowd of people outside No.17 and stopped to ask what was up. He was told, 'McKenna's killed his wife.' Billington knew all about McKenna's troubles and had no doubt seen him often enough in his father's pub drinking, and was aware of the constant rows that he had been having with his wife. He decided that discretion was the better part of valour, and as nothing could now be done for the poor woman, it was better if he left immediately, in case it damaged his chances of officiating in the execution!

Soon PC James Spencer was on the scene and he saw Anna McKenna, now dead, slumped into a chair near the door, with a wound in her throat. Her clothes were covered in blood and there was a deepening pool of blood on the floor. On the table was a bloodstained carving knife, and Emma McKenna sobbed out the events of the past fifteen minutes.

She had been cutting up some meat and when McKenna came in and saw his wife there, he seized the knife from Emma and threatened to cut Anna's head off. Showing considerable courage, Emma took the knife off him and put it back down on the table, making no attempt to hide it from the irate and drunken man in front of her.

McKenna burst out again to his wife, 'I suppose you took Palmer a cup of beer upstairs to him this morning and how do I know what he might have done to you? I'll cut your bloody throat for you!'

Seizing his arm, Emma managed to bundle her father-in-law out into the street and bolted the front door firmly behind him, but he soon returned and made another assault on the door. Emma, fearful of what McKenna might do in his rage, decided to unbolt the door and try to calm the angry man down. As the front door opened, Mckenna rushed towards his wife, who turned and ran into the back kitchen. Chasing after her, he grabbed his wife's shoulder and dragged her back into the front room, where she sat down in a chair, her eyes wild with fear. Seeing the knife on the table, McKenna picked it up and again shouted, 'You took Palmer a cup of beer up to him this morning, I'll cut your bloody throat,' and lunging forward he plunged the knife into his wife's throat and she sank back in the chair, uttering a dreadful moan, with blood shooting from a severed artery.

Emma also told the policeman that four days previously she had heard McKenna and his wife quarrelling and had seen McKenna and the lodger, Palmer, fighting on the floor. Palmer's wife had joined in the fight and Emma had tried to separate the combatants. 'Both McKenna and Palmer were drunk,' Emma said, although she went on to say that when they were sober, McKenna and his wife got on well (a state of affairs that applied to many working-class couples at that time).

After hearing this story PC Spencer hurried up Kestor Street to No. 5, looking for Patrick McKenna. At first the house seemed to be empty, but eventually he found the man cowering in a coalhole underneath the stairs. He had obviously been drinking and was in no state to resist the policeman when he reached in and grabbed his arm, asking him to come out. The policeman saw that McKenna was holding a penknife, with one blade open, which he quickly took from him, and half dragging McKenna he took him to the Spinner's Arms in Mill Hill Street, and from there sent for a cab to take them to the police station. Whilst they were waiting for the cab to come, Detectives Hart and Burrows arrived to give assistance and McKenna mumbled, 'She put the knife on the table and said, "Do it" and I said, "I will do for you."'

McKenna was obviously in no fit state to give a proper statement to the police at that time, but he continued, 'Is she dead? I am sorry. I had no intention of doing anything at that poor woman this morning.' Detective Burrows assisted PC Spencer in putting McKenna in the cab, and when they got to the police station McKenna said, 'It was an accident. I am sorry it happened. She dared me twice before I did it.' McKenna was put into the cells and left there overnight until he had sobered up sufficiently to provide a proper statement.

The body of the dead woman had meanwhile been taken to the mortuary, where Dr George Arthur Patrick performed a post-mortem. It disclosed that Anna McKenna was a well-nourished woman of about fifty-five years of age. She had some old bruises on her arms and there was a wound on the left side of the neck, about an inch long, below the jaw. The attack had severed the large artery, and her death had been caused by haemorrhaging.

Appearing in front of the magistrates, McKenna was committed to the Manchester Assizes. He appeared to be full of remorse for his crime and at the very short trial, in front of Mr Justice Bucknill, the judge summed up and told the jury that he would be delighted if they could find evidence to reduce the charge to manslaughter, advising them that they had to be sure that there was malice aforethought in McKenna's actions in order to return a verdict of 'Murder'. The jury, having heard the evidence, ignored the judge and took little time in bringing in a verdict of 'Murder', after which the judge passed the death sentence and McKenna was taken down.

The execution took place at Strangeways Prison on Tuesday, 3 December 1901, the executioner being James Billington, assisted by Henry Pierrepoint, father of the more famous Albert Pierrepoint. Billington was not a well man at the time and had been inclined to turn down the appointment, especially as he knew McKenna slightly. (He was not a close friend as some writers have maintained, and McKenna was probably better known to Billington's son, William.) However, it came to James Billington's attention that there was a rumour going round Bolton that he was frightened to execute his 'old pal', and because of this he decided to take the job. On the morning before the execution, James Billington was decidedly unwell, but his contract stipulated that he had to be inside the prison by 4 p.m. With minutes to spare he made it, and, together with Henry Pierrepoint, he went to the condemned cell to snatch a look at the prisoner through the peephole. McKenna, aged fifty-seven and seeming older, appeared to have been crying and looked a defeated man. As the two men watched, he got up and started pacing about the cell in an agitated manner. Later, whilst the two hangmen were having their regulation prison supper, Billington turned to his companion and muttered, 'Eh, Henry, I wish I'd never come.'

That evening, the hangman and his assistant were visited by the Prison Governor, who gave Billington the necessary information that would assist him in deciding upon the drop. McKenna was 5ft 10¼in in height and almost 11½ stone in weight and Billington, whose sole prerogative it was as the 'number one', fixed a drop of 6ft 7in.

The next morning, when they walked into the condemned cell, it was to find the prisoner weeping bitterly, and as McKenna was pinioned he again broke into tears, crying 'Lord help me.' He staggered as he shuffled towards the drop, where Pierrepoint rapidly strapped his feet. Within seconds he was hanging dead on the rope. Just before the trap gave way he shouted, 'Lord, have mercy upon me.'

William Billington was outside Bolton station to meet his father on his return from Manchester and shepherded him into a cab for the journey home. James Billington took to his bed and died eleven days later, the news appearing in the papers the following day, one of them unfortunately naming William as the deceased.

5

'I'LL DO IT! I'LL DO IT!'

Blackpool, 1903

The day of 9 March 1903 was a happy time for thirty-one-year-old Henry Bertram Starr, or it should have been, as this was the day on which he married Mary Hannah Blagg, his twenty-six-year-old girlfriend, at Christ Church, Blackpool. Starr had formerly been employed as a canvasser for an insurance company in Workington, and later in Clitheroe, but was now working as a labourer. Despite his comparatively lowly job, Bertram took good care of himself and on his marriage day his smart appearance belied his status. The marriage was perhaps not entirely of Starr's free will, as a daughter, Lilian, was born just five months later. Another hint that there was some friction was that Jane Blagg, Mary's mother, did not attend the ceremony, although she did permit the newlyweds to live with her at 76 Lord Street, a terraced street of two-up two-down cottages, running parallel to Dickson Road, North Shore.

Initially, the marriage appeared to be going well, but by the end of June 1903 Starr had begun drinking more than was good for him, and this provoked sharp words between Bertram and his bride. During July the position worsened and now Starr was threatening to hit his wife, despite her heavily pregnant state. The cause of this unpleasantness seemed to be that Mary kept tight hold of her money and steadfastly refused to waste any of it on providing her husband with alcohol.

'In that case,' Starr said, 'I'll knock it out of you.' Further rows resulted in Starr quitting his mother-in-law's house to stay with an aunt, leaving Mary in the last stages of her pregnancy and with nothing to live on, except for the £2 7s and six-pence that Starr handed over whilst she was in bed during her confinement.

One Sunday evening, Starr appeared at 76 Lord Street, although he did not enter the house, remaining in the vestibule, from where he shouted at his wife, 'Mary Hannah, you think I have been with other women and I have!' Later, there followed a series of letters between the two, Mary telling him that he had not a spark of love

Henry Bertram Starr from a contemporary newspaper. (Author's collection)

for her and that he had better stay away, as if he did appear, he would not gain admittance.

'If ever a man tried to put his wife in her grave,' she wrote, 'you have,' this letter being promptly returned, marked 'Returned with thanks. H.B.S.' Despite this, Starr continued to visit his wife and on 19 September, the two made things up and Mary Hannah left her mother's house to live with Starr and his aunt, probably on grounds of economy, as she could not work whilst her children were so young.

However, things again deteriorated and she was back with her mother by 1 November. At that time, Mary Hannah was so weak from the birth and lack of food that she could hardly manage to hold her baby without assistance. On 17 November, she received a letter in which Bertram wrote:

> My darling wife, I am very sorry indeed that you went away without telling me of your intention and can't express how keenly I feel in the matter. If you care to come back, I am quite willing to forget everything, but if it is your fixed purpose to live apart, then I must tell you that it is my intention to claim the custody of the child of our marriage within a few days after the receipt of this letter – I remain, yours affectionately, Henry B. Starr.

This was almost certainly an empty threat, and was presumably prompted by a newspaper cutting that he enclosed with the letter. Headed 'Veritas', it went on to say, 'Your wife cannot obtain a maintenance order against you so long as you are willing to receive her back. You are entitled to take the child and hold it against the whole world.' This 'advice' was completely spurious, but it persuaded Hannah to seek the help of a solicitor, Mr Callis, on 23 November, accompanied by her mother, the result of which was a magistrate's order for Starr to pay 6s per week for Hannah and her child, and that Hannah would have custody of her daughter. She also obtained a separation order against her husband. Later that evening, Starr was seen by a cabman muttering to himself, 'I'll do it! I'll do it!'

On Tuesday 24 November, Jane Blagg heard her daughter get up at about eight thirty to let the dog out, and ten minutes later the house was rent with shouts of 'Murder, Mother, Murder, Mother!' and she hurried downstairs to find Bertram Starr standing over her daughter, who was lying on the floor, hacking at her with a bread knife that he had picked up from the kitchen table.

As Jane Blagg stood, horrified at the scene, she saw Starr strike several blows. 'Harry, Harry,' (the name she usually called Starr) 'Whatever are you doing?'

Starr dropped the knife and ran into the next room, a scullery which led to the back door. Thinking that her son-in-law intended to leave the house, Jane followed him through in order to close the back door behind him, but instead he picked up a small dessert knife and with it stabbed her in the corner of her left eye. He followed this up with a further blow to Jane's neck and wrestled her to the floor, where he hit her several times on the head with his fists, leaving several large bruises.

'Harry, Harry,' the distraught woman cried to her attacker, 'Do let me go. You've done one, let me go for Hannah's sake.' At this, Starr stepped back and again made for the back door. Jane Blagg struggled to her feet, her head still spinning from the savage blows she had received, and fastened the door between the kitchen and scullery, sliding the bolt to prevent Starr coming back in again. Meanwhile, Starr had gone outside and had run off down the back street.

Jane then ran to the front door, still in her nightdress and screaming all the while, and saw a man coming towards her, a joiner named William Shackleton. 'He has murdered my wench. Come into my house and see,' she screamed at him, and he followed her in to see Mary Hannah lying, apparently dead, on the hearthrug, a small pool of blood seeping from her. Suddenly, the inert woman moaned and Shackleton hurried off to fetch Dr Johnson, who arrived shortly afterwards. He found the girl lying on her back across the hearthrug in the back kitchen, fully dressed except for her feet, which were bare. Her left arm was extended above her head and the right arm lay by her side, with both legs fully extended. There were several cuts on the woman's face and chest, one of which had penetrated the heart and had caused her death. In her left forearm were five more wounds and classic defence wounds on her left palm. Mary had obviously struggled violently during her tussle and had been wounded in twenty places, Dr Johnson saying that great force must have been used. Death was by internal haemorrhage.

Lying on the floor, about a foot from the body, was the broken blade of a knife, the handle to which was found on a table in the kitchen. Later, Mrs Blagg found a number of cigarette ends in the outside lavatory, which she assumed had been left by Starr during the night, and remembered that about midnight her dog had become restless, which he always did when there were strangers about. It looked

Mary Hannah Starr, from a contemporary newspaper. (Author's collection)

as though Starr had spent the night there, waiting for his wife to get up the next morning.

Soon afterwards, Police Sergeant William Greenwood arrived, and after inspecting the body saw it taken to the mortuary, where he examined the clothing. He found several cuts in a flannelette chest protector and the dead woman's chemise, which coincided with wounds on the body.

Meanwhile there was hue and cry for Bertram Starr, who appeared to have got clean away from the scene of the crime. The Chief Constable, Herbert E. Derham, communicated with his own, and the adjacent forces and men were sent out in all directions to look for the missing man. They found that he had first gone into the Derby Hotel, where barman Frederick Birchall supplied him with a glass of bitter, and then Starr asked for something to eat and if there was anywhere where he could clean himself up. Birchall said that food would be inconvenient because he would have to leave the bar unattended, and that there was nowhere the man could have a wash. Starr then bought a bottle of stout, which he drank, and then made his way to the Duke of York pub in Dickson Road, with the same requests for food and a place to wash. The barmaid, Melena Piggott, thought the man was rather nervous and excited and when she told him that it would not be possible to have a wash, he seemed to lose interest and went, leaving a bottle of stout untouched.

The next time Starr was seen was by the lavatory attendant at Talbot Square, who provided him with a wash and brush up. Starr told him that he had been out all night and had been fighting and the attendant then noticed that Starr's hands were covered in blood. Having cleaned himself up Starr made to leave the lavatory, just as PC William Lambert happened by, and the constable immediately spotted that Starr's cuffs appeared to be stained with blood and he also thought that the man had been drinking, although he was far from being drunk.

'Is your name Starr,' asked the policeman, who had already been warned about the murder before he set out on his beat.

'Yes,' was the reply. 'Is my wife dead? I'll go with you,' and after being handcuffed, he waited patiently whilst Lambert phoned for assistance. Together with Sergeant Butterworth, the constable took Starr to the police station by cab, where he was charged with murder.

The trial commenced on 7 December at Liverpool Assizes, before Mr Justice Ridley. Starr, looking smart as usual, did not go into the witness box and the prosecution, led by Mr Blackrod Wright, told the jury that the prisoner's mental state had been gone into and that he understood perfectly the nature of his act in killing his wife. A number of witnesses were called and Jane Blagg was particularly distressed when she went into the witness box to tell about her daughter's death. She identified the large ivory-handled bread knife with the blade broken off near the handle, which was said to be the murder weapon, and the smaller knife, which was a normal kitchen implement, the blade of which was bent nearly double.

The inevitable verdict was 'Guilty' and Starr received the death sentence without flinching, the judge telling him that it would be foolish to hope for mercy.

Modern-day view of Lord Street, Blackpool, where the Starrs lived. (A. Hayhurst)

The Duke of York, where Starr called in after the murder. (A. Hayhurst)

The execution took place at Walton Prison on Tuesday, 29 December 1903, in the presence of the Under Sheriff, the Deputy Governor of the prison, and the Chief Warder. The morning was dull and dark and the condemned man had spent a disturbed last night, so he was possibly relieved when John Billington and Henry Pierrepoint arrived at eight o'clock to usher him out of this world, his way being lit by lanterns carried by prison warders. Billington was 'number one', with Pierrepoint merely there to observe; this was part of his training for when he would later assume the position of Chief Executioner.

The condemned cell at Liverpool was some distance from the execution chamber and Starr had been brought to a more convenient cell to be pinioned. From here the walk to the gallows was only about fourteen yards. He walked to the scaffold apparently unconcerned, although it was noticed that he did shiver a little when he got out in the open air. On the trap Starr stood motionless, listening intently to the words of the priest reciting the prescribed verses, whilst Billington expertly adjusted the cap and noose. As the priest began the final words, 'O Lord Jesus Christ, Lamb of God, that takest away the sins of the world, have mercy upon him and receive his soul,' Billington pulled the lever to send Starr 6ft 10in to his doom, the tenth murderer to die on the gallows at Walton Gaol.

What the trial jury were not told was that Bertram Starr had been tried for his life on a previous occasion. In 1896, he had been tried at Manchester for the murder of his sweetheart, Elizabeth Coulthard, at Clitheroe, but was acquitted. It was reported that a year later he wrote some verses to Elizabeth's memory, verses that were said not to be without literary merit.

6

'THERE IS NONE LIKE ALICE TO ME'

Blackburn, 1912

Since the 1850s there had been a mill on the site between Copy Nook and Gate Street, Blackburn, but in 1886, just two years before the mysterious Jack the Ripper terrorised the East End of London, the old mill was demolished and a new one built. It was to have all the most modern machinery and promised lucrative employment for the workers who lived in the serried rows of terraced housing surrounding the mill. The mill, which boasted 570 looms, was owned by D. and W. Taylor and opened in 1887, Queen Victoria's golden jubilee year, so there were only two names to be considered for the new enterprise: 'Victoria' and 'Jubilee'. In the event 'Jubilee' won it, and so the mill was named. Although the building still stands today, it is no longer a mill and the only evidence of what it was built for is in the cast-iron lintel over the door.

At 54 Riley Street lived twenty-two-year-old Arthur Birkett, a weaver at the Jubilee mill. All who knew him said that he was a nice lad, hard working and the main support for his mother, who was a widow. They, with his grandmother and his young sister, all lived together in what must have been a rather cramped dwelling, only a few minutes' walk from the mill. For the past few weeks, Arthur had been 'walking out' (to use a local phrase) with eighteen-year-old Alice Beetham, who also worked at the mill, but Alice, it has to be said, was a little bit out of Arthur's league.

Although only a factory girl, Alice was a stunner and was considered to be the bonniest girl in the mill, with wide-set eyes, a broad face and inviting lips. She could not have earned a great deal of money at her work, but she was always well turned-out, and one photograph shows her dressed in a handsome outfit that must have been quite expensive. Another has her wearing one of the enormous hats that were all the rage at the time, so she was also a follower of fashion. Arthur Birkett must have thought that he had hit the jackpot when Alice first agreed to go out with him, after they met at the Easter Fair, but unfortunately for Arthur this happy state of affairs did not last long. Within four weeks, Alice had grown tired of her new boyfriend; perhaps he did not come up to her high expectations. She remarked to a friend, Mrs Lily Wagg, 'I can't be doing with that Arthur. He'll have to go.'

Lily, somewhat older than Alice, kept her counsel and said nothing. She had thought from the beginning that this striking young girl, who turned eyes everywhere she went, was never going to settle with a very ordinary weaver lad; she had her mind set on better things. However, for the time being the young couple continued to meet at Lily Wagg's house in Laurel Street, where they enjoyed a chat with Lily and her husband and occasionally all went out together.

It is possible that young Arthur had had some presentiment about his girlfriend's state of mind, for they had been to the cinema together to see a film about quarrelling lovers, and as they came out after the show he had said to her, 'We are not like that, are we Alice?' The girl merely shook her head and made no reply.

There is also a possibility that there were other influences on Alice, notably her father. The family were staunch Roman Catholic, whereas the Birketts were Protestants, and, whilst the affair between the two had only been going on for a short time, Mr Beetham had already made no secret of his dislike for Arthur. He had expressed a wish that Alice should have nothing to do with him, which in the short term, his daughter had ignored.

However, on Friday 17 May, Arthur and his girlfriend had words and later in the day he told Lily Wagg what had happened: 'She says that she doesn't want to go out with me any more,' he said, 'And before the end of the week, I'll cut her bloody head off!' Not for one moment believing that he would actually carry out his threat, Lily tried her best to calm him down.

'No,' he replied. 'If I can't have her, no-one will,' and there the conversation ended.

The following day, he sought out Lily at the mill and told her, 'Tell Alice to think nothing of what I said. I have been thinking things over and the next she gets, I hope she'll like.' Hearing this, Lily felt a lot happier about the situation and imagined that Arthur had come to terms with the loss of his girlfriend.

'There are lots more fish in the sea,' she said to him, by way of offering comfort, but instead of agreeing he replied, 'There is none like Alice to me,' and Lily began to think that maybe he had not accepted the position at all. Lily's husband had also heard the 'chopping' threat by Birkett, but did not think that he was serious about it.

On Monday morning, 20 May 1912, both Arthur and Alice went to the mill in time for the 6 a.m. start. Neither spoke to the other, but Birkett passed the time of day with another worker, Ellen Wilkinson. Seeing him look somewhat down in the mouth, she said cheerfully, 'You look crammed today, as if I had said something about you.' Birkett waved his hand in the direction of Alice. 'It's not you, it's her,' he muttered.

Ellen knew that the couple had been walking out together and asked, 'Have you been with her this weekend?'

Miss Alice Beetham. (By kind permission of Cotton Town Digitisation Project)

Arthur Birkett. (By kind permission of Cotton Town Digitisation Project)

Jubilee mill, as it is today. (A. Hayhurst)

'No,' was the reply. 'I think it is through her father. I have done wrong once; it does not say I have always done wrong.'*

'Never mind,' said Ellen, 'it will soon blow over.'

Three hours later a number of employees gathered in the weft room, including Alice and Arthur. Alice had a weft can under her left arm and was doing her best to avoid Birkett's glances. Suddenly, Birkett caught up with her and flung his left arm around her head, jerking it back and exposing her throat. There was a flash and a jet of blood sprayed out from Alice's throat. James Slater, another employee, attempted to separate the couple and Alice then collapsed on the floor. Birkett now turned the razor upon himself, inflicting two wounds in his throat, one on each side. He fell to the floor, face downwards, beside his victim. The whole incident had taken less than a minute.

One of the girls said later that she had seen Birkett say something to Alice, who replied to him, and then Birkett pulled out his razor and attacked her. At first, she thought that Birkett was going to kiss Alice and started giggling. On taking a second look, she saw the terrible wound in Alice's neck; her head had nearly been severed from her body. The other onlookers were horrified, and after a few moments of stunned silence someone gave the alarm and then tried to render first

---

* Quite what Birkett meant when he said 'I have done wrong' is not clear; there is no mention in the press, or at the subsequent trial, of any misdemeanour.

aid to the couple. The mill manager, Samuel Smith, appeared and gave instructions that Birkett and Alice should be carried into the mill yard and then telephoned the Copy Nook police station. Afterwards he went back to where Birkett was lying and attempted to put a bandage round his neck.

'You are making it too tight,' Birkett moaned.

'Where is the knife you used?' asked the manager.

'It is something sharper than a knife,' was the reply, and in response to Smith's question, 'Was it a razor?', Birkett said, 'Yes.' Smith immediately gave orders to another worker to go and find it. James Slater came out into the yard and crouched over Birkett's recumbent form. The man's lips moved and Slater bent lower to catch what he said: 'She struck me. You won't see me alive any more,' mumbled Birkett, and then went silent. Slater noted that his colleague's wounds did not seem very serious.

PC Walter Eddleston appeared and found the bodies lying about two yards away from one another. Satisfying himself that Alice was dead, he turned his attention to Birkett, who whispered, 'Take me away from here. Take me to the police station.'

'You do not have to say anything,' said the constable, 'but anything you do say may be taken down and used in evidence.' Birkett's eyes tried to focus. 'It's all through her father,' he said, before he was taken off to the infirmary in a horse ambulance. Someone then handed to the policeman an open razor that had been found on the mill floor, near where the bodies had lain.

In the ambulance, on his way to the hospital, Birkett told PC John Bellis, 'I have been off my head for two days. I have been crazy and did not know what I was doing.' Later, at the infirmary, he said, 'I did not intend to harm the girl; I only intended to take my own life. I walked about until one o'clock yesterday morning and when I saw Alice going for some weft this morning, I followed her and asked her to make it up, but she would not. I got hold of her and I do not remember what happened afterwards. I am very sorry for what happened.' He repeated this last sentence several times and then asked, 'Is she dead?', to which no one replied. Meanwhile, Alice's body had been taken to the mortuary. Inspector Garrett now took over charge of the case.

Alice's family – mother, father and her five siblings – were devastated and both parents were said to be in a state of collapse, while groups of women stood quietly in Billinge Street, whispering to one another. They had known Alice as a bright, cheerful girl and many of them had also known of her affair with Birkett. Back at the mill, the workers were in such a state of nervous exhaustion that the order was given for the mill to be closed for the day and the employees were sent home.

Birkett's mother, also in a state of collapse, told the *Manchester Evening Chronicle* that she could not tell how such a terrible thing had come to pass. 'My boy,' she

said, 'had said nothing at all to me, though I had noticed that he seemed very quiet and depressed for some days. He was as good a lad at home as you could wish for and he was passionately fond of Alice. The couple had come to my house for tea a couple of weeks ago and had seemed very fond of one another.'

An inquest on the dead girl was held on Tuesday 20 May, and the coroner, Mr H.J. Robinson, said that this was an enquiry into the death of an eighteen-year-old girl, who was killed by having her throat cut. Evidence of identification would be taken and then the inquest would be postponed to a future date, to take place at the Town Hall.

Thomas Edward Beetham, the dead girl's father, gave evidence that his daughter had been in good health and had worked at the Gate Street mill ever since she left school. He had not seen her on the day she died, as she usually left for work before he got up. After agreeing that he knew of Arthur Birkett, but had seen him only once, the coroner deferred the inquest until Friday 31 May. A paragraph in the local paper said that the murdered girl's funeral would take place on 25 May, and noted that Birkett was said to be improving in the infirmary and that his wounds were not life threatening.

The next Saturday was the day of the funeral and a great number of people crowded into Billinge Street, many of them carrying small bunches of flowers. Inside No.24, the coffin lay in the front kitchen surrounded by family wreaths and offerings from many of the dead girl's friends. There had been a collection at the Jubilee mill, some of which had been sent to the parents, with the rest going to a handsome wreath on behalf of all the workers.

The procession to the cemetery was timed to start at 2.15 p.m., and when the hearse arrived the coffin was laid reverently therein and surrounded by the floral tributes, which almost hid the coffin from view. Mrs Beetham was in an advanced state of distress, hardly being able to walk and had to be assisted to the coach, supported by her husband and the Catholic priest, Father Cobb. The priest asked for a glass of water to be brought for the distraught mother and some of the neighbours tried to persuade her to stay at home whilst her husband accompanied the coffin to the cemetery, but Mrs Beetham made a super-human effort and insisted that she would attend the funeral come what may.

In the first carriage rode Mr and Mrs Beetham with four of their children, the youngest one staying at home. All were deeply affected and many of the crowd in the street, both men and women, wept freely as the cortege moved away. Ten young women, workmates of the dead girl and dressed all in black, walked behind the hearse, carrying posies. In accordance with custom all blinds were drawn in Billinge Street and also along the route, an indication of how much the local populace had been affected by this dreadful murder. Just a few streets away from the Beetham home, the blinds were also drawn at the house of Arthur Birkett in Riley Street, but of Mrs Birkett there was no sign. As the procession moved along, thousands of people lined the route and men doffed their caps as the hearse moved slowly past.

Blackburn cemetery, where Alice lies in an unmarked grave. (A. Hayhurst)

The *Darwen News* carried a full account of the funeral, and noted that a shop window in the town showed a photograph of the dead girl, which was soon surrounded by sightseers. After a simple service in the Catholic chapel, the cortege moved to the graveside in section F of the cemetery, one reserved for those of the Roman Catholic faith. Mrs Beetham, now in a state of almost total collapse, was assisted to and from the grave with some difficulty.

The coroner's inquest resumed on 31 May, although no members of the public, apart from witnesses, were allowed into the courtroom. Amongst those present were the Chief Constable, Mr Isaac Lewis, Superintendent C. Hodson and Inspector Pomfret. Birkett was allowed to sit in the dock, looking pale and ill. The first witness to appear was Lily Wagg, who said that the young couple had been walking out together for about six weeks and had visited her house on a number of occasions. Three weeks before the tragedy, the couple had spent the afternoon and evening at her house, and a week before the murder they had gone to a picture house with Lily and her husband. Three days before the tragedy, Alice Beetham had confided in Lily that she was going to give Birkett up, although she did not give any reason.

'Did Birkett make any threat?' asked the coroner.

'Yes,' replied the witness, 'he said he would cut her head off.' She also told the coroner that at breakfast time, on the morning of the murder, Alice had told her that Birkett had stared at her but that she had tried to ignore him. She saw the couple go into the weft warehouse and then saw Birkett's attack on his former sweetheart, at which she fainted from the shock.

Police Surgeon, Dr Bannister, said that he had examined the body of the dead girl and found a deep incised wound 2½in behind the left ear to 2½in behind the right ear, all the way around the neck apart from 4in at the back. This could all have been done in one stroke, using considerable force. Birkett had suffered two incised wounds in the neck, the one on the right about half an inch deep, severing some of the muscles of the neck, but the left one merely superficial.

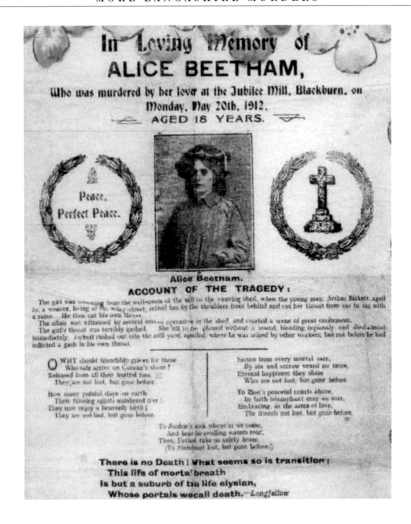

In Loving Memory of
ALICE BEETHAM,
Who was murdered by her lover at the Jubilee Mill, Blackburn, on
Monday, May 20th, 1912.
AGED 18 YEARS.

Peace,
Perfect Peace.

Alice Beetham.

ACCOUNT OF THE TRAGEDY:

The girl was passing from the weft-room of the mill to the weaving shed, when the young man, Arthur Birkett, aged 22, a weaver, living at 60, ——— street, seized her by the shoulders from behind and cut her throat from ear to ear with a razor. He then cut his own throat.
The affair was witnessed by several cotton operatives in the shed, and created a scene of great excitement. The girl's throat was terribly gashed. She fell to the ground without a sound, bleeding copiously, and died almost immediately. Birkett rushed out into the mill yard, spalled, where he was seized by other workers, but not before he had inflicted a gash in his own throat.

WHY should friendship grieve for those
    Who safe arrive on Canaan's shore?
Released from all their hurtful foes,
    They are not lost, but gone before.

How many painful days on earth
    Their fainting spirits numbered o'er!
They now enjoy a heavenly birth:
    They are not lost, but gone before.

Secure from every mortal care,
    By sin and sorrow vexed no more,
Eternal happiness they share,
    Who are not lost, but gone before.

To Zion's peaceful courts above,
    In faith triumphant may we soar,
Embracing, in the arms of love,
    The friends not lost, but gone before.

To Jordan's ank where'er we come,
    And hear he swelling waters roar,
Then, Father take us safely home
    (To friends not lost, but gone before.)

There is no Death! What seems so is transition:
    This life of mortal breath
Is but a suburb of the life elysian,
    Whose portals we call death.—*Longfellow*

Commemorative napkin for Alice Beetham. (By kind permission of Cotton Town Digitisation Project)

The coroner did not take long to sum up and the jury, without leaving the courtroom, came in with a verdict of 'Wilful Murder', and Arthur Birkett was then committed, on the coroner's warrant, to appear on trial at the next Manchester Assizes. Birkett slumped forward and had to be assisted from the dock. On 7 June Birkett was put before the magistrates on a charge of 'Wilful Murder'. It was noted that he was looking somewhat better than he had appeared at the inquest; with a bandage round his throat, he wore a jacket with a black tie and seemed composed.

Mr Prynne appeared for the prosecution and Mr Harry Blackhouse, a local lawyer, defended. Evidence given at the inquest was repeated, during which the accused man looked close to tears.

Lily Wagg told the court that when Birkett had come to her house on the Friday before the murder, he had seemed upset because his girl was throwing him over, and he was constantly biting his lip. Shortly after that, he had said that he would cut her head off. Lily Wagg had hardly got the words out of her mouth when the accused man was standing up in the dock, shouting, 'I said nothing of the sort!' The policeman who was sitting next to him in the dock gestured for him to sit down again, which he did.

Walter Wagg said that he had also heard Birkett threaten to chop Alice's head off, but when cross-examined he said that he did not think he meant it seriously. Several of the employees at the Jubilee mill then gave their own versions of the murder. During this hearing, Birkett said nothing and when the magistrates remanded him to appear at the next Assizes, he showed no sign of emotion.

The trial began on 8 July before Mr Justice Bucknill. Appearing for the prosecution were Gordon Hewart (later to become Lord Chief Justice, as Lord Hewart of Bury) and Mr A.R. Kennedy, while the defence was handled by Mr H. Lindon Riley. Birkett pleaded 'Not Guilty' in a calm voice and then Gordon Hewart told the court that the facts of the case were clear and it was difficult to see how the jury could come to any other conclusion than that Birkett had murdered Alice.

Once the prosecution witnesses had been heard, it was the turn of the defence. Birkett did not go into the witness box, and his lawyer immediately started to address the jury. He said that the jury had two alternatives, one that the accused was insane and the other, that the circumstances of the case entitled them to bring in a verdict of 'Manslaughter'. The judge then summed up and the jury were out for only sixteen minutes before returning a verdict of 'Guilty of Wilful Murder'. Mr Justice Bucknill pronounced the sentence of death and then Birkett turned to speak to his counsel. Having said just a few words, he fell down in a dead faint and had to be carried out of the dock.

In the fifteen days of life left to him, Birkett occupied himself writing letters to his family and must have been comforted when he was told that a petition for his reprieve had carried more than 60,000 signatures. These, however, were to be of no avail. In a letter to his parents Birkett wrote, 'I shall be waiting for you all in heaven and I hope I shall meet Alice. God bless her. I am wishing she likes me as much as I more than like her. I have not taken to anyone like her, but to think that it should come to this!'

He also requested that a photograph of the dead girl should be sent to him at the prison. His mother wrote a letter to Queen Mary, asking her to intercede for her son's life, telling Her Majesty that he was the main support of the household.

Birkett rose early on the morning of 23 July and dressed in the dark blue serge suit that he had worn at the trial. Resigned to his fate, he talked to the warders in a low voice, all the time looking at the picture of Alice which had been sent to him. Shortly before 8 a.m., executioner John Ellis entered the condemned cell with his assistant, Albert Lumb, and after pinioning the prisoner they led him the few short steps to the gallows. A large crowd had gathered outside the prison to await the notice of execution, which was duly posted on the main gate.

Long before the execution time, the Birkett's house in Riley Street was thronged with relatives and friends of the condemned man, and a considerable number

St Thomas' Church, where a memorial service was held for Birkett. (A. Hayhurst)

of floral tributes were delivered. The vicar, Reverend F.G. Chevassut, led a short service, and later a Salvation Army band arrived and another service took place in the street, during which Mrs Birkett, deeply upset, appeared at her front door. At the appointed hour, she and her family knelt in prayer whilst outside in the street her neighbours sang 'Nearer my God to Thee'. Mr Birkett was even more overcome than his wife and had to receive the attentions of a nurse in the back room. According to the *Manchester Evening News*, Mrs Beetham was amongst those who attended the service.

Conforming to a local custom, souvenir napkins were printed bearing a photograph of the dead girl and a short account of the tragedy. Similar ones had been circulated after a pit disaster at Wigan in 1910 and the sinking of the *Titanic* in 1912. The members of the St Thomas' Conservative Club subscribed to a miniature monument, standing 18in high and covered by a glass dome, which was presented to Mrs Birkett. The inscription read, 'In loving memory of Arthur Birkett, born July 27th 1889, died July 23rd 1912. Son, thy sins are forgiven thee.'

7

DEATH ON THE DUNES

Lytham St Annes, 1919

Lieutenant Frederick Rothwell Holt, of the 4th Battalion Loyal North Yorkshire Regiment, had been called up early in the First World War as a territorial officer. Originally the territorials were committed only to fighting in this country, but the rule was soon amended and most territorials volunteered to serve abroad, as did Frederick (known as Eric) Holt. He fought in the notorious Ypres salient at the battle of Festubert; a small village to the south of Neuve Chapelle, in what was intended to be the first British army night-attack in the First World War. The battle, as usual, was preceded by a tremendous three-day bombardment by hundreds of guns, which fired off over 100,000 shells; this, if nothing else, warned the enemy that a major attack was coming. This hurricane of shells, however, made little impact on the German lines, which were often buried 40ft down in the chalk, safe from all but the most direct hits, but the weather, for once, was good and the initial advance by mainly Indian troops made some progress. The battle raged from the 15 to 27 May, and although the village of Festubert was ultimately captured, the British divisions had suffered heavy casualties and had to be withdrawn.

It was possibly his experiences at Festubert that resulted in Holt being invalided out of the army in 1915, suffering from depression, and he spent the rest of the war working in the Malay States, returning to his native Lancashire in 1918.

Of medium build, with a rather large nose underneath which was a neatly clipped moustache, Holt's friends generally regarded him as being a genial companion, always up for a good time, but rather excitable. Shortly after his return to England, he met and fell in love with a woman named Kathleen Elsie Harriet Breaks, usually known as Kitty, who, although married, had parted from her husband within months of the marriage and now regarded herself as virtually single, although she had not obtained a divorce. Kitty was a very attractive woman and always dressed immaculately, and she also, it seemed, was not short of men

Frederick Rothwell Holt. (Author's collection)

friends. There was some mystery about her marriage and it later transpired that Kitty had never lived with her husband after the wedding, although they had gone on holidays together, and when her husband, John Stoddart Breaks, travelled to motor shows around the country, Kitty often accompanied him. Moreover, the fact of the marriage had been kept from Kitty's parents for over three years, and when they eventually found out they were naturally distressed and angry at the deception.

At first, Kitty was hopelessly infatuated with Holt and they talked of obtaining a cottage in which they could live together, but by January 1919 the affair seemed to be cooling, at least on Holt's part, whilst Kitty still remained keen. Holt started to ignore her frequent letters and she wrote to him in March 1919 that his silence hurt her very much indeed. The argument, if that is what it was, sorted itself out and in May 1919 Holt applied for an insurance policy in the sum of £10,000 on their joint lives with the Atlas Insurance company, the proposal describing Mrs Breaks as aged 26, married, living at the Cleveland Club, Middlesborough and as being a typist and bookkeeper. In order to secure this policy, Holt wrote to the insurance company saying, 'With regard to Mrs Breaks' proposal, you will notice that she has written that she is married, the reason being that she is not sure whether she is a widow or not, although she has received notice from the War Office to the effect that her husband is missing, believed killed.'

The company demanded further information, which Holt supplied, to the effect that the object of the insurance was to make provision for himself and family and it would also be useful for a possible marriage settlement. He proposed to pay both premiums himself and in the event of his death, the money was to go to Mrs Breaks, and in the case of her death, to him.

Kitty queried the necessity for the policy and, in particular, the huge sum involved, which would mean a premium well above her ability to afford, but Holt wrote to her saying, 'We must go in for a lot whilst we are at it. I am hoping that they will insure us both for the same amount.'

On 19 July Kitty left her job at the club and, from then on, she had no paid occupation. She was now living in Bradford, where her lover sent her sums of money from time to time. Holt himself had inherited the sum of £500 per annum but was overdrawn at the bank in the sum of £1,254, although the bank held securities to the value of £1,300 in support.

On 19 August, the superintendent of the insurance company wrote to Holt saying that he did not think that his directors would accept the proposal because Holt did not have an insurable interest in the life of Mrs Breaks.[*]

Some days later, Holt was informed that the company had refused the policy, although they added that should their marriage take place, they would be pleased to reconsider.

Meanwhile, the love affair continue although the two were living apart, and, in September, after meeting Holt in Bradford, Kitty wrote to him saying, 'I don't really know how to thank you for the glorious, happy time I spent with you. Somehow, you just seem to make life worth living for me.'

Holt now seems to have convinced her that life insurance was important, for on 16 October she paid the first premium of a Royal London Insurance policy for £5,000 on her own life, amounting to £105 12s 6d (all of which had been given to her by Holt); and she received the policy later in November. All the time the correspondence between them continued, Kitty waxing lyrical about her lover's attributes, describing him as 'just the biggest, whitest man I know', and sometimes referring to him as 'Superman'.

On 17 December Kitty Breaks went to her solicitor to enquire about making a will, in Holt's favour, and that day wrote to him explaining, 'There is little news except that I want to be near you.' This prompted Holt to visit Kitty again – she was still in Bradford – and he was now replying promptly to her letters, writing, 'My dear, darling Kathleen, you have no idea how lonely I feel without you ... I am so longing for Christmas. I am sure that there will be a day someday when we will never part.' This final sentence seems odd, for as Kitty was unemployed and was staying in lodgings, there does not seem to have been any reason for them to remain apart, unless Holt wished it.

On 20 December 1919, Holt again visited Kitty and on the following day she went to her solicitors to sign her will. Except for two small bequests, she left all the £5,000 for which she was now insured, plus her wedding ring, to Holt. Her clothes and jewellery she left to her sister, Muriel. On the following day, Holt and Kitty went by train from Bradford to Blackpool, where Kitty booked into the Palatine Hotel, whilst Holt spent the night at his parents' house in nearby Lytham St Annes.

The next evening, Kitty sat down to dinner in her hotel at about twenty minutes past eight. The waitress who served her said later that Kitty had eaten little and

---

[*] The murder, by the infamous Dr Palmer of Rugeley, of several members of his family and friends in the 1850s, after he had taken out substantial insurance cover on them, had led to alterations in the law, and whilst a policyholder could take out unlimited insurance on his/her own life or on the life of a spouse, the law did and does not recognise other classes of natural affection.

looked rather preoccupied. Finishing her meal at around 9 p.m., Kitty got up and left the hotel to catch a tram towards Lytham. She did not return, and her body was discovered on the sand hills at Lytham St Annes the following morning, about 200 yards north of the Manchester Convalescent Home, by a farmer, named Gillet, who said that he had followed footprints in the sand.

Kitty Breaks had been shot three times, although there appeared to be no signs of a struggle. There were footprints of a man and a woman at the scene, and a man's footprints leading away from the body. A post-mortem examination disclosed that the fatal injury was caused by a bullet entering at the back of the left-hand side of the head, which had passed downwards and inwards, exiting under the right side of the chin. Death would have been practically instantaneous, said Dr Kellcott. There were three other wounds behind the left shoulder, but none of these would have been fatal. There was also a lacerated wound 1¼in long at the top of the head, probably caused by a blunt instrument. In the opinion of Dr Kellcott, the bullet wounds were all caused whilst the victim was in the prone position. Dr Blair, who assisted Dr Kellcott, said that she was probably standing when the blow to the head was struck and she fell on her back. He commented particularly that the night of the murder had been very dark and that there had been four hits from four shots.

Lying by the side of the dead body was a woman's handbag, obviously belonging to Kitty, containing two letters; one from a man named Tom and another written in pencil on the notepaper of the Midland Hotel, Bradford, which read:

Tom, Many thanks for your letter received after the evening we spent the other night. Tom, you have misunderstood me, or else you would never have written to me as you did. I was surprised at your letter and please do not write to me in that strain again. You ask for my friendship and I thank you, but it is impossible. However there is no reason why we should not be just friends ... Some day we may come across each other and have a few minutes together, but you must never approach that subject again as you did in your letter. If you do so, we must not see each other again. Believe me, yours most sincerely.

The letter was undated and unsigned and the identity of the mysterious Tom was never discovered, although there were suspicions that it might have been Holt. The handbag also contained a wedding ring, a gold mounted cigarette holder, a cheque book, a diary, a dinner bill, a receipt for left luggage, 25s in cash and two scent bottles on which were the initials 'K.E.B.' and 'F.R.H.'

Amongst the footprints found around the body, the police took the impression of a man's shoes which appeared to have been repaired. A further search revealed a man's left hand glove, which bore bloodstains. The companion to this glove was discovered a few days later, as was a revolver; both of which were handed in to the police.

The police were very quickly on the trail of Holt, aided by a tram driver, John Mills, who had known Holt for a number of years and who had seen him alight at a stop only a few yards from the murder scene at around half past nine, the approximate

Lake Road, Lytham, where Holt lived with his parents. (A. Hayhurst)

The sand hills where Kitty Breaks met her end. (A. Hayhurst)

time that Kitty Breaks must have arrived there. Later, at about 10.30 p.m., the same driver saw Holt standing at the tram stop to make the return journey, although he could not be certain whether Holt had actually boarded his tram.

Early on Christmas Day, Inspector Sherlock arrived at the house of Holt's parents and told Holt that he was making enquiries into the death of Mrs Breaks. Holt did not seem to be discomfited or surprised by this announcement and agreed to make a statement, in which he said that he had left Kitty at the railway station and had not seen her after that. He had gone to the Clifton Hotel on Christmas Eve to book a table for two for lunch at 1.30 p.m. The waiter saw him sitting there on his own and passed a remark about his friend not having turned up.

'I'm going to the bar for a drink,' replied Holt, 'let me know when Miss Breaks arrives,' and a while later he dined alone. He also mentioned that he had lost a pair of gloves.

During the interview, Inspector Sherlock formed the impression that Holt was lying and he also noticed a recent scratch on Holt's right wrist and four scratches on his left cheek. When questioned about these, Holt coolly said that the scratch on his wrist might have been done by a dog or a cat and that the marks on his cheek he had done with his razor. Holt was arrested on suspicion of the murder of Kitty Breaks and taken to the police station, where on 26 December Dr Kellcott examined him and asked him about the various scratches on his body. Holt repeated his statement that the wrist wound was caused by a dog and the rest by his razor, and at the hearing before the magistrates on 23 January 1920, Dr Kellcott admitted that the marks could certainly have been done in the manner that the accused suggested.

Evidence was given that the revolver, which had been found only a short distance away from the footprints in the sand, had been manufactured in Birmingham by the firm Webley & Scott. The serial number on the outside of the weapon had been filed away, but there was another on the inside of the revolver, number 99,362. Such a numbered revolver had been sold to an officer in the army on 10 August 1914 and had been signed for by 'F.R. Holt'.

Benjamin Crabtree, superintendent in charge of the Prudential Assurance Company's office in Bradford, gave evidence that the previous September Holt had approached him to discuss a policy on his life for £10,000. He had asked if there would be any increase in the premium if he went to live abroad and he also wanted to know if the company issued policies on female lives, as his fiancée was thinking about taking out a policy for £5,000. These were considerable sums at the time and would have produced significant commission for the agent handling the transactions. Holt was, in fact, an accredited insurance agent.

The superintendent queried if Holt's fiancée would be able to afford the not inconsiderable premiums and Holt remarked, 'I could pay them myself, if necessary,' to which Mr Crabtree replied, 'That would be unlawful and would not be allowed.' Holt then left and that was the last Crabtree had seen of him. An official from the Royal London Insurance Company told the court that he had accepted an insurance proposal from Mrs Breaks and she had paid the premium with her own cheque.

Edward Marshall Hall. (Author's collection)

Once all the evidence had been heard, the magistrates adjourned for only a few minutes before coming back and committing the accused man for trial. Holt then stood up and, before he was taken to the cells, read the following statement in a clear and steady voice:

> I am not guilty. I was never on the scene of the murder. I left the deceased lady in the train at Ansdell [a suburb of Lytham St Annes] at twenty minutes past seven upon the night of December 22 last. I never saw her again. She had arranged to meet me at the Clifton Hotel at half past twelve on the following morning. I kept the appointment, but she did not appear.

Despite his overdrawn position at the bank, which was backed up by share certificates, Holt had other securities available totaling over £1,200. With this, he was able to obtain the services of one of the most formidable defence lawyers of the time, Sir Edward Marshall Hall. Knighted in 1917, Hall was a handsome, imposing figure, although something of a hypochondriac. His entry into court would be proceeded by a junior bearing smelling salts and bottles of medicine, a box of pills, a nasal spray and often an inflatable rubber ring – he suffered badly from haemorrhoids. None of this, however, distracted him from the job in hand and he was a master of the histrionic movement and meaningful phrase, and there were many who thought that Hall would have made just as much money on the stage as he did from the law.

The trial began in Manchester on 23 February 1920 before Mr Justice Greer. Sir Gordon Hewart KC, now the Attorney-General, led for the prosecution, assisted by Mr Merryman KC and Mr Jordan, whilst for the defence, Marshall Hall appeared with Mr Wingate Saul KC and Mr McKeever.

Immediately, Marshall Hall requested that a jury should be formed to consider the mental state of the accused man. This was agreed and Captain Dawes, of the War Office, produced Holt's war record, which disclosed that he had reported sick after the Battle of Festubert, suffering from depression and loss of confidence and also had rheumatism, which was said to affect his mental state. He was marked unfit for duty and a month later, fit for light duty. He faced another board of enquiry in February 1916 and it was found that he was suffering from

Mr Justice Greer. (Author's collection)

headaches, an impaired memory and poor concentration. Holt listened to the catalogue of his ailments without moving a muscle, almost as if he were a medical student listening to a lecture.

Reference was made to a document that Holt had written whilst he was awaiting trial, in which he stated that he was being tracked by dogs in his cell, tormented by fever in the form of flies and shot at with bullets filled with mercury whilst he lay full-length on his bed. Holt's solicitor, Mr Woosnam, stated that he had seen this document and it caused him to think that his client was mentally deranged.

Next to appear was Dr Robert Percy Smith, formerly superintendent of the Bethlehem (Bedlam) Hospital in London. He was considered to be an expert on forms of insanity and he had interviewed the accused whilst he was in Strangeways Prison. Dr Smith formed the opinion that Holt was of unsound mind, due to delusional insanity, but had to admit, under cross-examination, that a statement which Holt had made to the police on 24 December proclaiming his innocence showed no sign of insanity at all. In reply to Gordon Hewart's question, 'Is it your view that he was perfectly sane on December 24 and insane on December 25?' Smith replied simply, 'Yes.' Whilst this might well have been a concept that could be understood by lawyers, it was not understood by many in the courtroom, including some of the jury. Smith went on to say that while the accused was aware that a charge of murder was laid against him, he was very doubtful if Holt was intelligent enough to follow the evidence of the witnesses. This again was an unhelpful and confusing statement from a defence witness.

Dr Ernest S. Reynolds, visiting surgeon at Cheadle Royal Asylum, agreed with the two previous witnesses. He said that whilst interviewing Holt, the accused described two sorts of flies visiting him, some larger than others and one lot were all blown away when he blew his nose! In his opinion, Holt had the facial appearance to be found in cases of mental degeneracy: narrow forehead, eyes close together and prominent ears, something that he noticed as soon as he was introduced to the accused.

For the prosecution were called the Governor of Preston Prison, Major Norman Burrows; Mr W.T. Watts, a warder in the same prison; the Governor of Strangeways Prison; Dr Walter Francis Moore, medical officer of Preston Prison; and Dr Stanley Howard Shannon, medical officer of Strangeways Prison. All gave evidence that they noticed nothing abnormal in Holt's behaviour during the time he had been in prison.

After a short retirement, the verdict of the jury was that the accused was fit to plead, and after a fresh jury was empanelled the trial proper began. Holt, dressed in a brown lounge suit, apparently unmoved by this turn of events, sat quietly in the dock with his arms folded, glancing round the court as the jury was sworn in. Every available square foot of space in the court was taken up when Sir Gordon Hewart rose to commence the case for the prosecution:

> The motive for this murder was Holt's efforts to insure himself and the dead woman for very large sums. You will probably come to the conclusion that it was never the prisoner's intention to insure himself at all, nor did he do so. Was it not manifest that the insurance of Mrs Breaks was to be carried out at Holt's instigation and for his benefit? That completed the project that the prisoner began and so diligently carried out. To complete the scheme, it was necessary for Mrs Breaks to make a will in his favour – she did so.

Various letters were then read out, including one from Holt to Kitty saying, 'I feel that some time there will be no parting. I wonder whether it will be after our tour in France, or when, but I am sure there will be a day when we shall never part.'

It might have struck the jury as odd that if these two people were so deeply in love, as they professed to each other to be, why they just did not live together. The fact that Kitty Breaks was still legally married was an impediment, but not insurmountable and although such behaviour was frowned upon in polite circles at that time, Holt was of independent means and he could have afforded to ignore the outside world and be happy with his mistress.

The Manchester Assizes. (Author's collection)

Caricature of Sir Gordon Hewart. (Author's collection)

'On the afternoon of December 22nd,' the Attorney-General continued, 'after staying the night with the accused, Mrs Breaks went to her solicitors and executed the will, leaving almost everything to her lover, including most of the proceeds of her life policy should she predecease him. Holt was evidently waiting for her and together they took the train towards Blackpool, where Kitty alighted, Holt having left the train at Ansdell.'

Then Hewart began to trace Holt's movements on the evening of 23 December. He suggested that Holt went home and changed his coat and was wearing a Burberry when he went out again. He described a pair of wet and sandy shoes that had been found in Holt's room when the police called, and these, together with the shoes that Kitty Breaks had been wearing, were placed in the impressions found in the sand and were found to be an exact fit. Regarding the gloves which had been discarded near the body, 'Might it not have been,' the Attorney-General suggested, 'that one glove was taken off to fire the revolver and, having dropped one glove, he reflected that it would not do for him to be found with the other glove alone and so threw it away. A revolver had been found in Holt's bedroom, but it was a Colt, not a Webley, and unconnected with the crime. The Webley found near the scene had been proved to belong to Holt and appeared to have been casually discarded.'

Concluding his speech, the Attorney-General summed up: 'The gloves – his gloves – how did they come to be there? The revolver – his revolver – how did it come to be there? The footprints – his footprints – how did they come to be there?' With every word, Sir Gordon Hewart was driving another nail into Holt's coffin. 'What was the inference suggested by the fact that the woman went in the night, in the dark and rain, to those sand hills? The footprints showed that she walked some distance with someone. Was it not obvious that it was someone she trusted completely? She chose to accompany that man and was felled by a blow on the back of the head and four bullets were fired into her hapless body.' He asked the jury to find that the man was Frederick Rothwell Holt.

John Stoddart Breaks, Kitty's husband, told the court that he had last seen his wife in October 1919, when he had been driving his car and she flagged him down. She got in and they had a short run before he turned round and dropped her at the spot where she had first seen him. He said that his wife, with whom he was on friendly terms, was tearful at the time of their meeting and they 'talked things over', but made no arrangements to meet again.

Other witnesses repeated their evidence given at the Magistrate's Court and in evidence for the defence, Frederick Holt, the father of the accused, stated that his wife's father had been in an asylum and was very excitable and irritable. His (the father's) first wife's aunt had died in Cheadle Asylum and the accused, his son, was very nervous and rather dull and stupid. (This did not really square up to a man who had been in the Territorial Army and who had attained commissioned rank.)

'After he came home from Malaya,' said his father, 'he was very moody and sometimes would sit in front of the fire without taking any notice of anybody. He just seemed to be thinking. That continued up to the present time. On the night of the murder, my son returned home at 8.15 p.m. and coming into the drawing room said, "How Do! Any letters?" On being handed them, he read them and then went upstairs. He left the house again at about 8.45 p.m. and came back in at about 9.45. Told that supper would be ready shortly after 10 p.m., he went out again and returned at about 10.10, when he had his supper and went to bed.'

The following day, the accused man had his breakfast at 10 a.m. He then took the shoes he had been wearing the previous night and cleaned them. The shoes produced in court (and which fitted the footprints found by the body) were not his son's.

If what his father said was true, then Holt had an unassailable alibi, but Sir Gordon Hewart soon dealt with that: 'Have you ever come across that familiar kind of alibi which describes something that truly happened, but not on the occasion when it is said to have happened?' he said to Holt's father.

'I know what an alibi is,' was the reply.

'Somebody in your household had his supper about half past eleven that night?'

'My youngest son,' answered Holt's father.

'Are you sure it was your youngest son?'

'Positive.'

'Are you prepared to say that there were no shoes in the accused's room that morning [the 24th] that were wet?' Hewart persisted.

'I never examined any shoes,' was the reply. Mrs Holt, the prisoner's stepmother, and Minnie Holt, his sister, gave evidence in corroboration of Holt seniors's statement.

Sir Edward Marshall Hall's speech for the defence took two and a half hours. His opening shot, glancing at the public gallery

Kitty Breaks' estranged husband. (Author's collection)

that was crowded with women, was, 'It makes one feel sick for the femininity of this country that women should come in their dozens day-by-day to gloat over the trouble of a man on trial for his life.' He was rewarded by hisses from the 'femininity' present. He continued:

> If what the prosecution had said were true, the jury was facing a story dealing with the most appalling crime it was possible to imagine. He did not suppose that there could be a worse crime than that of a man who under the guise of making passionate love to a lovely woman, was merely keeping her quiet until the moment came when he could murder her and put the proceeds of her insurance in his pocket. According to the theory of the prosecution, Holt proceeded without hesitation or wavering, learning what he must do to get Mrs Breaks to make a will in his favour and he induced the woman to go to the sand hills between 9.30 and 10 at night and there murdered her. It was in an area where everybody knew him, where he had been resident for several years, where the police and tram drivers knew him and where he must, if the prosecution was right, have been hanging about for a couple of hours to murder her in an atrocious manner, leaving gloves and revolver and footmarks and going back to his home with the certainty of detection. I say that the theory of the prosecution is grossly impossible. If the jury accepted the theory of the prosecution, Holt must have known that his letters were in her handbag and that everyone in St Annes and Blackpool could have found out that his association with the dead woman was of long standing.

Turning to Holt's father's evidence, he went on, 'Did they believe that Mr Holt senior, the stepmother and the sister, had come there deliberately to perjure themselves in order to save this man's life? The crime, by whoever it was committed, was committed by no sane man. The jury had been told that the accused was sane. Therefore, he could not have done the murder.'

He pointed out to the jury that the Webley revolver had not been traced to Holt's possession since 1914 and during the five days of the trial, the only disinterested spectator was the man in the dock. The man was suffering from some sort of delusional insanity and the only defence the prisoner had made and stuck to from the beginning was that he was not guilty.

The Attorney-General spoke for nearly two hours and said that the suggestion that the accused was insane on the night of the murder required far more of a complete testimony than the sporadic references that had been made to it. A suggestion had been made that no human mind could be so diabolical as to form a project in May to be carried out in December, but the prisoner did not intend it to last until December – here he turned and stared at the jury – it took him some time to discover that he had no insurable interest in Mrs Breaks.

The judge summed up and referred to an affectionate letter written by the prisoner to the dead woman on 18 December. This, he said, seemed to be a letter from a man who prized his association with the woman, but strange things happened in human life and it was not impossible that a man might fall out of love with a woman, which might enable him, when the time came, to commit a crime of this kind. Two defences had been put forward, insanity and alibi, but they did not run very well together in harness. If the jury found the accused Not Guilty on the ground of insanity, they would have to state that ground and the prisoner would be detained as a criminal lunatic. There was a remarkable absence of evidence, he said, in support of the plea of insanity.

The jury was absent for just under an hour and in response to the question 'Do you find Frederick Rothwell Holt Guilty or Not Guilty?' the foreman of the jury said, without hesitation, 'Guilty.' Holt heard the sentence of death without emotion, turned, and walked down the steps to the cells, hands in pockets.

An appeal was heard before the Lord Chief Justice of England, Earl Reading, but had little chance of success. After a patient hearing, the Earl said, 'We have had a great deal more evidence of theory, very little of fact, little that added to the knowledge before the jury and we come to the conclusion that there is no ground for impugning the verdict. The result is that the appeal must be dismissed.'

The Home Secretary caused the usual enquiry to be made about Holt's state of mind, but it did not help, neither did a petition addressed to him saying, 'Your petitioners are of the opinion and humbly beg to submit that Frederick Rothwell Holt did not commit the said murder (if he committed it at all) for any purpose of gain, but in an uncontrollable fit of jealous passion and in a state of madness, and that we most seriously doubt whether said Frederick Rothwell Holt is now in his right mind.'

Mr Wingate Saul applied for a medical examination on Holt to see if he was suffering from syphilis and/or insanity. He claimed that examination of the cerebrospinal fluid would be the only means of finding out if Holt had early cerebral disease. This request was thrown out by the appeal judges.

At 8 a.m. on Tuesday, 13 April 1920, John Ellis and his assistant, William Willis, entered the condemned cell at Manchester Prison, when Holt, who until now had seemed his usual calm, stoical self, began to struggle violently. It needed four warders to contain him whilst the straps were put on and then, with some difficulty, they got him on to the gallows.

After the execution, the revolver that had been shown in evidence remained in the hands of the police, but Marshall Hall insisted that he had been made a gift of it by the executed man's father and demanded that it should be given to him. Harry Lane (Later Sir Harry), Chief Constable of Lancashire, refused to hand it over and Marshall Hall told him that he intended to sue under the Police Property Act, and also claim costs. Mr Lane replied saying that he was sorry, but handing the revolver over would create a precedent and anyway, it was the invariable practice in the Lancashire force for the police to retain such property. After further correspondence, Chief Constable Lane appeared to be getting rather tired of the arrogant way in which Marshall Hall was seeking to over-ride his decision and he made his feelings plain in a letter dated 13 October 1920, when he wrote:

I was not aware that the revolver referred to had been given to you and I might also point out that never at any time during the deceased's trial did you, the prisoner or his relatives claim or admit that the revolver was his. I submitted the matter to the Home Office and was instructed to hand over exhibits in connection with the case, with the exception of the Webley revolver. This was not handed over, and except on an order of a Magistrate under the Police Property Act 1897, and until such an order is made, I do not propose to hand over the revolver to anyone. With regard to your allegation that it was offered as a memento to the Attorney-General, I have no knowledge of such; the revolver is in the possession of the police and has never been offered to anyone with my consent.

Two days later Hall wrote:

I am not accustomed to have statements of mine described as 'allegations'. It was not until after the trial that the revolver was given to me and as the jury found it was Holt's revolver, the property in it at his death passed to his father, as his personal representative and it was he who instructed Mr Woosnam [Holt's solicitor] to give it to me.

The spat ultimately reached the Home Secretary, the Right Honorable Edward Shortt KC, who replied to Hall saying, 'Sorry I can't help,' and there the matter ended.

On 21 February 1921, *The Times* wrote, 'The will dated June 23. 1911 of Frederick R. Holt, commission agent, of Lake Road, Ansdell, Lancashire, who died at Strangeways, Manchester on April 13 last has now been probated. Estate was sworn at £203 gross. Net personalty nil.'

8

FOURPENCE FOR ICE CREAM

Salford, 1924

The dictionary definition of the word wastrel is 'a good-for-nothing person', and this description fitted twenty-three-year-old John Charles Horner very accurately. He was born in Pendleton, Salford to respectable working-class parents and lived with them at 15 Lissadell Street, Pendleton. He was the third of four children and, like his siblings, he attended Frederick Road School, leaving at the age of fourteen to work for the Pendleton Co-operative Society as a milk boy. After two years, he left to 'better himself' and went to work for Messrs Mandlebergs of Cobden Street, Pendleton, leaving there after a year to take up a position with Messrs Locketts, where he stayed for seven months.

It appears that Horner's work during this time was satisfactory. On leaving Locketts, he joined the Royal Navy and was discharged in May 1919, his character being described as 'good'. However, from then on, things started to go downhill and in July 1919, he enlisted in the Royal Field Artillery. While in the service he was punished for robbing a comrade and was finally discharged in 1921 'with ignominy'.

He returned to live with his parents, and his father, wishing to give his boy the best chance he could, bought him a horse and cart to help him earn an honest living. Hard work now seemed to become anathema to young Horner and he neglected his work to such an extent that his exasperated father sold the horse and cart and left him to his own devices. Thereafter, he was in and out of the hands of the Salford County Borough Police and appeared before the magistrates on numerous occasions, for offences such as 'stealing a £1 note', 'stealing a bicycle', 'burglary' and being 'drunk and disorderly', which resulted in total sentences of thirteen months in gaol. At his final appearance in court, before the crime that was to end his life, he appeared to have sunk to the depths of depravity, accused of robbing his father of money and jewellery and of taking all the lead off his father's stable roof. For this he was given six months in gaol, being released in March 1924.

In the early summer of 1924, Horner was working for Messrs Brooks (bakers) Ltd as a van driver, a position that he had obtained by lying about his qualifications. Someone may have tipped his employer off, for they began to make enquiries about him, something that came to Horner's attention. He then absconded with £38 of his employer's takings and was sacked; the police were soon informed.

On 10 June 1924, the local police received a complaint from a Mrs Sarah Goulden, who said that he had indecently exposed himself to her, and when the sergeant suggested that she try to identify the culprit she had no trouble in giving a recognisable description of Horner. If only the police had taken immediate action on that complaint, two lives might have been saved.

The morning of 10 June had started off badly. Although it was Whit Tuesday and a public holiday, the skies were overcast, there was intermittent rain and a biting wind blew, even though it was nearing mid-summer. At 3 p.m. that afternoon, Horner had made arrangements to see his girlfriend, Sarah Verity, a ward maid at a local hospital, but when this time arrived, Sarah seems to have put her head out of the door, seen that it was raining heavily, and decided that she would not go out in that for anybody! Besides, she had an informal arrangement with Horner that if she could not meet him at their usual place, the railway station at Old Trafford, he would come to the hospital to see her at her afternoon tea break. The two had known each other for seven years, being virtually childhood sweethearts, and had conducted a desultory on/off relationship during that time.

Despite the weather, five-year-old Norman Widdowson Pinchin, known in the neighbourhood as 'Copper' due to his ginger hair, was playing happily with his friend, eight-year-old Eric Wilson, outside his home at 9 Crescent View, Salford. The rain was falling intermittently and the two young lads took advantage of the sunshine, when it came, to run about. After seeking permission from Norman's father, the two boys went into nearby Peel Park, an open recreational space which ran north-south alongside the River Irwell. The park was a popular 'green lung' for the people of the Salford area, one of three public parks that had been opened on 22 August 1846, paid for by public subscription. At the time of this story, Laurence S. Lowry was studying art at Salford Royal Technical College, which overlooked the park.

Entering the park, the two boys ran down some stone steps into what was known as the 'summer shed', a low building where people could take their ease and perhaps listen to a band. There was quite a crowd of people in the vicinity and as the boys played, a man came up to them, and, feeling in his pocket, he pulled out four pennies, which he handed to Eric Wilson, suggesting that he should go and buy two ice cream wafers. At the same time, he made a lewd remark to the two young lads, the meaning of which neither appeared to understand and anyway, the lure of the two ices being offered was certainly more interesting to them.

The trio made their way out of Peel Park and walked towards Windsor Bridge, which spanned the canal. On the bridge was a small shop, Hardmans, which sold ice creams among other things. Eric went into the shop, leaving the man and Norman walking on towards the canal towpath, which ran under the bridge.

Peel Park, Salford. (By kind permission of Salford Local History Library)

Duck Pond, from Terrace Steps, Peel Park, Salford

Another view of Peel Park. (By kind permission of Salford Local History Library)

Having bought the ice creams, Eric came out of the shop and looked for his friend, but neither Norman nor the man was in sight. Just then, it started to rain and Eric abandoned all thought of finding his young friend and went home to 10 Oakfield Terrace, finishing off both ice creams as he went.

At about ten minutes to four, Harry Barnes, a slinger with J.H. Ashton Timber Merchants, was perched on a baulk of timber, looking over the canal wall, which at that point was about 12ft in height. He was on the lookout for the paperboy, who he was expecting to see any minute with the sixth edition of the *One O'Clock*, a local newssheet. Suddenly, he noticed a young boy wearing a light pair of trousers with a greenish jersey, walking hand-in-hand with a man. They were walking along the towpath towards Windsor Bridge and then disappeared from sight as they walked underneath the bridge. Barnes thought little of it, mentally cursing the newsboy for being late with the racing results, but about nine minutes later he saw the duo again. This time, the man was grasping the boy's clothing at the back and to Barnes' surprise, the man suddenly stepped forward and threw him into the canal. Barnes saw that the boy had disappeared under the water and the man knelt down, apparently looking to see if the boy would surface; when he did not, the man got up and walked on.

Hardly believing the evidence of his own eyes, Barnes scrambled down from his perch on the wall and ran towards the wicket gate, which gave access on to the canal. Gesturing to the commissionaire, whose job it was to tend to the gate, he ran through and towards the Windsor Bridge, seeing the man coming towards him, but the man walked past him without saying a word. Barnes went on to the spot where he had seen the boy thrown into the water, but there was no sign of him and he straightened up and retraced his steps, passing through the canal gate into Walness Road, where he saw the man in front of him. Keeping a safe distance away from the man, who was wearing a dark blue overcoat and a trilby hat, Barnes followed him along the Crescent (which ran east from the Windsor Bridge), until he saw two men who he knew were police officers, although at the time they were not in uniform.

Crossing over the road he blurted out his story, after which one of the policemen, Walter Smith, went across the road and ran after the man, who was stopped and asked, 'Have you seen anything of a little boy dressed in a blue or green jersey?'

'No,' answered the man.

'Well,' said the policeman, gesturing at Harry Barnes who was standing across the road, 'a man over there says you have just thrown a little boy dressed in such a jersey into the canal.'

The man stood sullenly and said nothing. Barnes and the other policeman, PC Lawrence, then joined them and the four men walked back until they reached the towpath by the Windsor Bridge.

Barnes then pointed to the water and said, 'I have seen this man throw a little boy dressed in a blue or green jersey, with light trousers on, into the canal here.'

The man reacted immediately, shouting, 'Nothing of the sort!' and at the same time attempted to hit his accuser. This assault was quickly stopped by the policemen,

The canal towpath, looking towards the Windsor Bridge. Wallness Road is behind the wall on the left. (By kind permission of Salford Local History Library)

who then took the man, John Charles Horner, to the Cross Lane police station. Later, Barnes took the police photographer to the spot where he had seen the young boy thrown into the water, but there was still no sign of him. PC Smith returned to the canal side later in the afternoon, bringing with him a set of grappling irons which he used to drag the canal. Within a short time, the hooks had made contact and, pulling on the rope, Smith drew to the surface the body of a young boy. He was wearing a blue jersey and his trousers were missing, although his braces were still on underneath the jersey. Despite a feeling that the boy was past all help, the constable performed artificial respiration until he was sure that there was no point in continuing further and, after summoning an ambulance, took the body to the Pendleton mortuary.

The following day the body was examined by Dr Stanley Hodgson, who found that there were no external signs of violence on the body, but considered that the boy had been the subject of a savage sexual attack and that the shock of this had killed him. He was further of the opinion that the boy had probably been dead before his body hit the water. He had determined that the canal was a 'hot-water' canal and, therefore, the shock of immersion would not have killed him. A week later, Constable Henry Barlow was sent to the canal with the grappling irons and pulled out a pair of boys' light-brown sports trousers, which the boy's father later confirmed were those belonging to his dead son.

A police line-up was arranged at Salford Town Hall and ten men, including Horner, were assembled, but when asked, Horner objected to one man, who was told to stand down. Detective Inspector William Jowatt asked Horner if he was

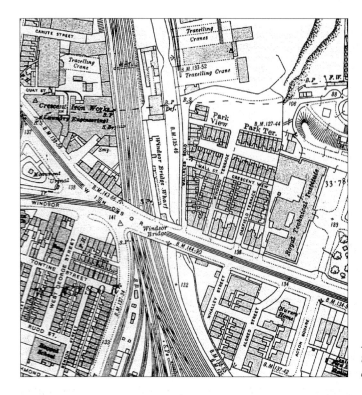

A contemporary map of the crime scene. (Author's collection)

now satisfied with the arrangements and he said that he would prefer to have a wash first. This request was granted and he came back a few minutes later, choosing the second from the right as his place in the line.

The first witness to come in was Eric Wilson, who walked along the line until he came to Horner. Wilson touched him and said, without any hesitation, 'This is him.' After the young boy had been led out, Horner was offered the opportunity to change his position, but he declined and the second witness entered. This was Norman Thomas, a fourteen-year-old boy who had told the police that he had seen Norman Pinchin in Park View at around four o'clock, walking hand-in-hand with a man. Thomas identified Horner with as much certainty as the witness before him.

The usual hearings were conducted in the Magistrates' and Coroners' Courts and Eric Wilson was questioned closely at the coroner's hearing. He said that he had left his friend Norman and the man at the entrance to Peel Park, before going for the ice creams. Mention was also made of the lewd suggestion that the man had made to him. 'Did he ask you to let him do something to you?' said counsel.

'He did not ask if he could do something to me,' was the reply. However, at the magistrate's hearing a day later, the young boy admitted that the man had said something to him. It was to become clear that eight-year-old Eric was completely out of his depth in the imposing surroundings of the courtroom, and much of his evidence at the trial was at sixes and sevens with what he had said earlier. The same was to apply to other young witnesses.

The trial itself commenced on 17 July 1924 before Mr Justice Talbot. For the prosecution were William Madden and Hugh Beazley, whilst Mr McKeever acted for Horner. The trial, at times, almost lapsed into farce, mainly due to the youth of the main witnesses and their failure to understand what exactly they were doing in court. It was also difficult for them to remember what had taken place and the order in which it had happened. Horner pleaded Not Guilty to the charge of murder, and after evidence about the taking of police photographs, Harold Pinchin was the first witness. He described the clothes that his child had on when he went out to play on 10 June and confirmed that the trousers fished out of the canal were his son's.

Eric Wilson was next and in view of his young age, eight years and a fortnight, Mr Madden took great pains to elicit from him that he knew what he was in court for and that he knew that he had to speak the truth. When he said that he did not know what an oath was, the judge ruled that the boy could be examined without being sworn.

Mr Madden took the young witness through all the stages of the incident, during which the boy pointed to Horner in the dock and said, 'That's him.' He repeated the lewd words that Horner had said to him and his friend, although he did not seem to understand what the words meant. His whole focus was on the offer of two twopenny ice creams. The eight-year-old's other evidence was also a jumble of fact and fiction.

'Do you know the name of the street where the ice cream shop was?' questioned Madden.

'Number 10 Norfolk Terrace,' was the reply.

'Denver Terrace?' queried Madden.

'Yes.'

'And what is the name of the shop?'

'Horton's.'

'Do you mean Hardman's?'

'Yes.'

The judge then asked if Mr Pinchin was still in court and Mr Pinchin stood up. 'Do you know the name of the street that this boy mentions?'

'Yes,' said Pinchin, 'it would be Park View he would be going along.'

Here, the judge seemed perturbed that the prosecution lawyer was correcting the young witness. He leaned over and spoke to Eric Wilson. 'Just tell us again what the name of the street is.'

The reply came straight away, '10, Oldfield Terrace.' Defence counsel intervened. 'I think he means Oakfield.' The judge, glancing down at the plan in front of him, nodded. The boy then explained that after he had bought the ice creams, it had started to rain, so he had eaten both of them and hurried home. This time, he got the name of the street right.

It was then the turn of defence counsel, Mr McKeever, to cross-examine. 'Now, Eric,' he started, 'you have to wear spectacles?' The boy agreed and McKeever continued, 'That is because your sight is not very good, I suppose?'

'Yes.' (The prosecution made no attempt to establish that Eric might well have had excellent sight whilst wearing his glasses.) The boy repeated his evidence concerning meeting the accused and going off to buy the ice creams. There was now more confusion about where he had actually been. According to the witness, he had been in Crescent View when he saw Horner and the little boy, hand-in-hand, going into Hall Street, which led to the canal towpath gate, but he was adamant that he had not been near the canal.

'Were you in Crescent View?' asked McKeever.

'Yes.'

'But the canal is only a few yards down there, is it not?'

Again, the witness agreed. Counsel then referred to the magistrate's hearing. 'At the first court, when you said that you left a man and Norman at the park gates, that was not quite correct, was it?'

'No.'

'And you did not mention that the man had said something to you at that hearing?'

'No,' replied the eight-year-old witness, who by now was in some difficulty. He plainly did not understand what he was doing in the courtroom and his memory of events and names of streets had been shown to be faulty, which was hardly to be wondered at. The judge was clearly at fault in not dealing with this earlier; allowing a child to be questioned with as much rigour as an adult did the prosecution no favours and, indeed, might well have been helpful to the defence.

There was then more confusion thrown into the evidence when McKeever moved on to the words that the accused was said to have said to the two boys. 'Had you heard anyone else use those words?'

'Yes,' the boy replied.

'Who?' counsel shot back.

'Someone in our street.'

'A woman?'

'Yes,' replied the boy.

'Was that someone who lives near you?'

'Yes.'

'When did she say this to you,' continued McKeever.

'The day the little boy got drownded [sic].'

'What did she say when she used these words to you?'

By now, the young witness was becoming totally confused. 'I don't know,' he replied.

'But you remember she did come and say those words?' McKeever persisted.

'No,' said the boy and the interrogation then took on an almost surreal twist. 'She said to me, "I have got no friend now."'

'Then what did she say?' asked counsel.

'She did not say anything else.'

At this stage, McKeever gave up and moved on to another point. The witness agreed that when he had attended the line-up, the prisoner looked a bit frightened, whereas the other men in the line-up did not. (This was a disgraceful bit of leading by McKeever, which the judge did nothing to stifle. Quite how any eight year old could have been expected to describe that sort of emotion in circumstances that were entirely alien to him, was a mystery.)

Counsel went on, referring to the line-up, 'You knew Horner had been accused of something?'

'Yes,' Eric agreed.

'You could tell that the other men in the line-up did not care?'

'No,' was Eric's confused reply.

'You could see that easily, could you not?'

'Yes,' the boy replied.

McKeever sat down, presumably satisfied with the way he had effectively shown to the court that this witness was completely unreliable. Prosecuting counsel stood up and, pointing to the dock, said, 'Just look at that man there. Are you sure that is the man who spoke to you and went off with the little boy?'

'Quite sure,' was the reply, and there the little boy's interrogation ended.

The next witness was fourteen-year-old Norman Thomas, who confirmed that he had seen the accused with Norman Pinchin, walking hand-in-hand towards the canal at about 4 p.m. on Park View. Later that day, he had decided to go to the police station to tell what he had seen.

'Did you give a description of the man you had seen?' McKeever asked.

'Yes,' Norman confirmed.

'Did the policeman write it down?' replied McKeever.

'No,' said the witness.

McKeever looked shocked. 'He did not?' he said, his voice rising.

'No, Sir.'

Counsel looked puzzled. 'The little boy Eric Wilson says they did not go on to the canal bank the way you say at all, and he ought to know, he was with them. The little boy says they went down Crescent View and then down Hall Street, opposite the canal gate.'

'They could not possibly go down there,' retorted Norman Thomas. Then followed another bizarre moment, with argument between counsel and witness as to which exit (from Peel Park) Horner and the little boy had come. The matter was still not resolved when Norman Thomas was released, although the witness did agree with McKeever's statement that they could have gone down Windsor Terrace and then into Hall Street and then onto the towpath via the gate.

The next witness was Harry Barnes, the wood-yard employee, who had been responsible for pointing out Horner to the police. He said that he had seen Horner and the boy on the towpath.

'In what position were they walking,' asked Madden. 'Who was nearest the canal?'

'The prisoner,' was the reply.

'You could see the man?' interjected the judge, and the witness agreed.

'You could see who he was?' the judge persisted.

'No,' said Barnes.

'Then do not say the prisoner,' the judge said, sternly. This was the first time that he had said anything designed to clarify a point during the whole hearing. The witness then described the couple walking towards the Windsor Bridge and disappearing under the bridge. Nine minutes later, he saw Horner holding the little boy by the back and then throwing him into the canal. The witness revealed how he had left his workplace and had gone on to the towpath, where he saw Horner coming towards him, eventually passing him, heading for the gate.

'That was the first time you had seen his face?' he was asked.

'Yes, Sir.'

'What happened next?'

'I passed him without speaking and went to the canal to see if I could see the little boy. I could see no trace of him, so I turned back and followed the prisoner, who had by now gone through the Walness Gate,' said Barnes.

The judge intervened again, 'When you turned back, he was out of your sight, was he?' The witness confirmed this.

Counsel continued. 'When you got through the gate into Walness Road, you saw him again?'

'Yes, Sir.'

'Walking in which direction?'

'Towards the Crescent,' asserted Barnes.

'And you followed him?'

'Yes, to very near the fire station, on the Crescent.' Then followed how he had spotted the two policemen and had handed Horner over to them.

Defence counsel, Mr McKeever, commenced by trying to discredit the witness, hinting that he had been acting as a bookie's runner, rather than waiting for a newspaper to arrive. This the witness denied strenuously. He agreed that he thought that he had seen a tragedy occurring when he saw the man throw the little boy into the water.

'Why then,' McKeever asked, 'did you not drop off the wall on to the canal bank [a drop of 12ft] and keep the man in sight, running along the canal bank; instead of which you applied to the gateman for permission to leave the premises, losing perhaps a minute before you could take up the pursuit?'

'I used my own discretion,' was the reply.

'You say that you passed the man on the canal bank without speaking to him?' persisted McKeever.

'Yes,' confirmed Barnes.

'I put it to you that you passed him because you were not sure in your own mind that this was the man who had thrown the child in the canal.'

'There was nobody else on the canal bank,' replied the witness.

'There was no-one else on the canal bank, so you came to that conclusion,' McKeever said in a loud voice, staring at the jury. 'But at the time you first passed the prisoner on the canal bank, you surely did not think he was the murderer, or you would not have passed him?'

'There was nobody else on the canal bank.'

'That is what you think,' snorted McKeever.

The judge interjected, 'Did you say that it was only when you came back you lost sight of him? You never lost sight of him between the time you saw him throw the body in the water and the time you passed him without speaking?'

'Yes,' Barnes stated.

At this, McKeever burst out in frustration, 'Mr Barnes, how could you possibly have seen him all the time, when you came down from the wooden staging on the inside of the wall?'

'I have explained,' Barnes said limply, 'a minute elapsed.'

'Never mind the minute,' counsel snapped. 'During the time you were getting permission to leave the yard and the time the commissionaire was opening the wicket gate for you, the man was out of your sight – must have been, there was a 12ft wall between you.'

At last, Barnes got the message. 'Certainly he was out of my sight for a minute.'

'So he might have gone anywhere?' said the counsel.

'It was the same overcoat I saw and the same trilby,' protested Barnes.

'If this man really had just committed such a crime as this, there would have been nothing to prevent him jumping on to a tramcar going in the other direction?' McKeever rejoined.

'No, Sir.'

Then came details of Horner's arrest, backed by appearances in the witness box from Constables Smith and Lawrence and, again, there were discrepancies that needed to be ironed out. The cross-examination by Mr McKeever of Constable Smith came first. 'When you approached the prisoner, did you say to him, "We are having some awful weather,"' began McKeever.

'I did not, Sir.'

'And did you ask him where he was going?'

'No, Sir.'

'Did he say to you he was going to the Salford Royal Hospital?'

'He did not, Sir.'

McKeever pressed on. 'And then did you ask him "What for?"'

'No, Sir.'

'And did you say to him, "What, like that?"'

'No, Sir.'

'And then did you say to him that he was drunk?'

'Nothing at all like that, Sir.'

'What did you say, then?'

'Have you seen anything of a little boy in a blue or green jersey?' Smith reported.

Once more the judge leaned forward. 'Do you mean that this is the first thing you said?'

'Yes, my Lord,' confirmed Smith.

McKeever went on. 'I put it to you that he did tell you he was going to Salford Royal Hospital to see his girl.'

'He did not say that.'

This question and denial system of interrogation was getting the court nowhere, and the constable also denied that he made any enquiries whatsoever about a girl at the hospital, saying, 'It did not occur to me to make enquiries. The accused is not speaking the truth because he did not say that to me at the time.'

'But when he was at the canal with you, he was so indignant at the charge Barnes made that he rushed at him and tried to strike him?'

Smith would not allow even this remark to pass unchallenged. 'Not so much indignant,' he said. Soon after, the trial adjourned for lunch, and when it resumed Constable Lawrence, in a few short sentences, backed up his colleague's evidence.

Presently, it was time for the defence, and the first witness was the accused man himself. He confirmed his identity, his age and also the fact that he had two brothers and a sister (although what possible relevance this could have to the case was not clear). He said that his girlfriend, Sarah Verity, was a ward maid at the Salford Royal Hospital, and that Tuesday was her half-day off. He told the court that he had arranged to meet her at Old Trafford railway station at three o'clock that afternoon. Horner arrived at five to three, but when his girlfriend had not shown up ten minutes later, he said, he went to Salford Docks and boarded a tramcar to the Palace Theatre on Cross Lane. There he found another tram, which would take him past Salford Royal, and he got off at the corner of Oldfield Road and Chapel Street, almost opposite the hospital, and looked up at the window from which his girl usually showed herself, but she was not there. Thinking that he might see her when she was on her tea break, at about 4 p.m. (it was then about 3.25) he walked down Oldfield Road to the canal and up to the Walness Road Gate, where he met Harry Barnes, about four yards from the gate. Neither man spoke and Horner said that he then walked along Walness Road until he reached the Crescent, where he continued walking in the Manchester direction until he reached the main gates of Peel Park. There, he was confronted by the policeman, who said something to him about the poor spell of weather they were having. He did not know the man, nor did he know that he was a policeman. The man then asked him where he was going, which Horner said felt strange, as he could not see why this should be of any interest to the man, but he answered that he was going to see his girl at Salford Royal. The other constable then came up with Barnes and Constable Smith and said that he had reason to believe that Horner had just thrown a young boy into the canal. 'Never!' said Horner and the quartet then made their way back to the Windsor Bridge, where Barnes accused him of putting the boy in the water and Horner said, 'Nothing of the kind!' and attempted to hit Barnes, being restrained by one of the policemen. He was then taken to Cross Lane police station and detained. Later he was put on an identity parade and two young boys picked him out from a row of nine men.

'There was,' he said, 'no truth in the statement that he had been in Peel Park that afternoon.' The walk that he had taken from the hospital to the canal was a favourite one for him and his girl and they had often walked that way. The prosecution counsel then got from Horner that when he was placed under arrest, his clothes were not taken from him and he continued to wear the same clothes, including an undershirt and other things, for over a week before a member of his family brought in some clean clothes and took the soiled ones home for washing. By the time of the trial, he was again wearing the same clothes that he had on when he was arrested.

Whilst Horner was telling his story, his voice fell to little more than a mumble and Mr Madden complained to the judge that he could not hear what the witness was saying. 'Speak up, will you?' the judge admonished him, and the questioning continued, with Horner admitting that he knew Peel Park and that the last time he had been there was with his girlfriend, on the Tuesday before the murder. When questioned as to why he had waited only ten minutes at the station, he said that he and his girl had an arrangement that if it was raining, she would not come and he would then go to the hospital and meet her there.

Eric Wilson was then brought into the well of the court and Horner was instructed to look at him. 'Just look at that little boy,' thundered William Madden. 'Will you swear that you did not see him in the park?'

'Yes,' replied Horner.

'Or in the summer shed?'

'Yes,' Horner repeated.

Madden then asked the accused if he had ever been in the summer shed, to which he answered, 'Not to my knowledge.'

'Then you were not in it on 10 June?' said Madden.

'No, Sir.'

'You have heard that little boy swear you were?' (This was incorrect, as young Wilson had not been sworn due to his tender age.)

Horner agreed and Madden continued, 'And that you spoke to him and made a nasty suggestion?'

'I have heard him say that, Sir,' was Horner's reply.

'And you have heard the other boy, Thomas, swear that he saw you pass by, holding the little boy's hand?'

'I heard him swear that, yes.'

Summing up Horner's story so far, Mr Madden put it that Horner claimed to have come from the Oldfield Road side of the Windsor Bridge and began to make his way back to the hospital, and that he had never gone under the bridge itself.

Then it was the turn of Sarah Verity to go into the witness box. Her name was called, but there was no reply. The name was called again and this time, Horner gestured from the dock towards a young lady sitting in the well of the court. This, it transpired, was Sarah Verity, who had been quietly following the evidence as it was given to the court. The fact that she should not have been listening to the evidence before she gave her own was overlooked and she went into the witness box. As it turned out, she had little to say. She had known the prisoner for a long time and there had been an agreement for the two to meet on 10 June at Old Trafford station, but because the rain was 'pelting down', she had not gone. Such arrangements to meet had been made 'many a time' she said, and that was the end of her evidence.

Mr McKeever then addressed the jury on behalf of the defence, and Mr Madden reciprocated for the prosecution, then Mr Justice Talbot began a long and careful summing up.

> The jury knew very well the cause of this boy's death, despite initial police feelings that he had drowned. The boy had been brutally treated and it was from such treatment that he died of shock. So far as the moral guilt of the man was concerned, it did not matter whether the boy had died from shock or drowning. The man, whoever he was, had treated the boy with no more compunction than if he had been a dead dog. There could be no doubt but that the outrage upon the boy was a felony and if anyone was found guilty of it, they would be liable to life imprisonment if the boy had lived. However, the law was that if by an act of felonious violence a person was killed, then whoever did it was guilty of an act of murder.

He went on to say that it was the job of the prosecution to prove, to the jury's satisfaction, beyond all reasonable serious doubt, that the man in the dock was the one who had committed the crime. Referring to the evidence of Eric Wilson, the judge said:

> I need not tell you, ladies and gentlemen, that the evidence of a child of that age is to be received with some degree of caution. The child [referring to children generally] as we know, is very prone to answer 'Yes' to questions it does not thoroughly understand and it is impossible to test the evidence of a child in the way in which the evidence of an adult can be tested. Indeed, it is impossible for counsel, whatever their ability, to cross-examine a child with any very great effect.

However, the judge left little doubt in the mind of the jury that Eric Wilson's account of the events of 10 June could be taken seriously and that there was ample independent corroboration of it. The fact that witnesses differed as to whether the accused and the little boy went down via Park View or Hall Street was not material, but it was right to call the jury's attention to the discrepancy. Wilson had also picked out the man at the police line-up.

Turning to the evidence of Norman Thomas, the judge said:

> He seems to be a very intelligent, clear-spoken boy, who said that he had seen the accused and Norman Pinchin walking hand-in-hand on the day of the murder, coming along Park Terrace and walking towards the canal. He was later confronted with the man at the police station and picked him out without hesitation. Harry Barnes had had clear sight of both sides of the canal and had seen no other persons at the time the accused and the little boy had walked past him. 'I saw them go underneath the bridge,' he said. And about nine minutes later, he saw the two

reappear and the accused throwing the little boy into the canal. There was no doubt that somebody did drop this body into the canal and there is no doubt whatsoever that Barnes saw it done.

Regarding the re-examination, Judge Talbot said, 'The witness has told you that on all the occasions he saw the man he had on a blue overcoat and a trilby hat, and it is the account of both Barnes and the prisoner that no single human being, except this man and the little boy, was seen there at that time on that afternoon.'

Later, the judge said that although Sarah Verity had told the court that she had agreed to meet the accused at three o'clock at Old Trafford station, she had not given proof that he was actually there at that time. Finally, the judge told the jury, 'You must be satisfied of a man's guilt before you can convict him, but if you are satisfied that he is the man who caused the death of this boy in the way in which his death was caused, then undoubtedly it is your duty to find him guilty of murder.'

The jury went out at 4.48 p.m. and returned one hour and two minutes later with a 'Guilty' verdict. Solemnly, the judge adjusted his black cap and pronounced a sentence of death.

The execution date was fixed for 13 August and the Chief Executioner, William Willis, and his assistant, Robert Wilson, were advised of the date by post. Each replied to the Governor of Strangeways Prison that they were available. Horner was refused permission to appeal, on the grounds that the only point at issue during his trial was that of identity, and there was ample evidence on which the jury could find that Horner was the guilty man.

An envelope arrived at the prison addressed to the condemned man, which the prison authorities naturally opened. It contained a strip of paper, seemingly torn from a sheet of brown paper, and written in ink were these words:

> I did the canal affair sorry to say and I came down to Liverpool and am going to America. When I was in Manchester I used to see you often you would pass for my brother no wonder they swore to you well I could not help it they are a lot of lunatics [*sic*].

The letter was unsigned and undated. This was either somebody's idea of a bizarre joke or else a poor attempt to throw doubt on Horner's guilt, but the Governor merely sent the missive on to the Home Office without further comment. No action was taken.

The condemned man was probably not aware that not only was his correspondence referred to the Home Office, but also anything he said whilst he was awaiting execution and which could have any bearing at all on his case. A letter to the Home Office, dated 11 August, now in the National Archives, noted, 'In the condemned cell diary yesterday, the following entry occurs. Prisoner stated "I would not mind if they reprieved me. I would then have fifteen years to do – it would soon pass."'

A further note said, 'At his visit today, the prisoner was asked point blank by his mother if he had committed the crime. The prisoner replied that he had not done

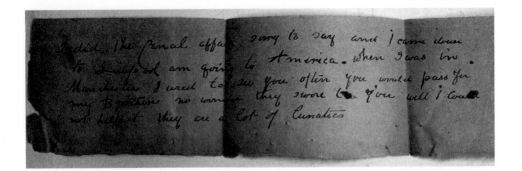

The anonymous note sent to the Governor of Strangeways Prison, claiming to have come from the real killer. (National Archives)

it.' Another letter, written in almost copperplate handwriting, and addressed to the Prison Medical Officer, read as follows:

> I respectfully bring to your notice the undermentioned statement, made to me this morning by prisoner 5253F Barlow. 'After 9 p.m. on June 14, prisoner 7055 Horner stated he was in Pendlebury on Saturday June 7 and drinking in company with a nurse, an actress and another fellow. After 10 p.m. they took away with them plenty of drink to a neighbouring house, staying there until 3 a.m. in the morning. On the Sunday, Horner gave his brother £10 for a present, proceeding to Preston on the Monday. On Tuesday morning, he met a discharged prisoner called Keo, just out that morning. They travelled together as far as Pendleton, when Keo went on to Salford. Horner gave him 10s. He writes a letter to his young lady on Saturday, asking her to come and see him next Tuesday, if she does not come, he says he will "Give the lot up, far better to be strung up." Horner also states that he will not tell any of these bastards anything [referring to the prison staff]. If Mr Riordan [a warder] gives him any chances, he will crack him with a chamber pot. Mr Wylde too, will get something on his head. He might as well get hung for two or three of them.' [*sic*]

This letter produced no action, other than an acknowledgement from the Home Office, and perhaps really amounted to nothing more than hearsay, but it could also be an indication of the sort of things that were going through Horner's mind about the time of the murder.

On 6 August, just seven days before the execution date, the Home Office received an eight-page letter from Horner's father, setting out reasons why his son should be reprieved. 'In the first instance,' wrote Mr Horner, 'the first interview my son had with his barrister, Mr McKeever, only took place the day before his trial, for about ten minutes – a very short time in which to prepare all details for his defence.' Another point made was that the two young prosecution witnesses had been able to see Horner being arrested on the towpath, which made it much easier for them to pick him out from the line-up. He also wrote:

I am also anxious that you should have the following facts before you, when considering his case. My son's character had been very good [supported by a letter from the Accountant General of the Navy] until an accident, when he received a blow to the head, which perforated an eardrum and led to his discharge from the navy. He then joined the Royal Artillery, but his 'old complaint' returned and thereafter he was often punished for disobeying orders on parade, because he was unable to hear the commands. On one occasion, when home on leave, he was very distressed about being punished so often and said that his fellow soldiers had suggested that he should steal something and so obtain his discharge. He stole £1 from a chum and was fined, but not discharged. The second time, he stole a bicycle and got three months, but this time he was also discharged with ignominy.

One evening, we went out and when we returned, Charles had gone to bed. When we went upstairs, we found him in his bedroom, which was full of gas. He had turned the gas tap on and only our timely return saved him.

On one of the occasions that Charles had been in prison, the Court Missionary had been to see Mr Horner and had asked him if he thought his son was 'right in the head?' These and other instances of odd behaviour were, his father thought, grounds for seeking a reprieve. On 9 August, however, the chairman of the Prison Commissioners received a letter from the Home Secretary, saying that the law must take its course.

At about this time, a newspaper article printed an interview with Sarah Verity, who said that she went to a party with Horner when, without warning or cause, he suddenly struck her. 'I was not indignant,' she told the reporter, 'because he was remorseful. He tried to excuse himself and he was exaggerated in his apologies. Then when I decided to forget the incident, he told me that he had pains in his head.'

On the afternoon of the day before the execution, William Willis and Robert Wilson, hangman and assistant, looking like respectable businessmen, entered the prison and went to the execution suite at the end of B wing, in the central area of the prison. Strangeways was one of the few prisons to have a permanent gallows and, in total, there were 100 executions carried out within its walls. Having tested the drop and satisfied themselves that everything was in order for the morrow, they settled down to have their tea and the pint of beer each that they were allowed under the regulations.

Early on the morning of 13 August, a crowd began to gather in front of Strangeways Prison and, according to the *Manchester Evening News*, many of them were women in clogs and shawls. Horner's father, mother and eldest brother had been to see him for the last time two days before, and his mother had been allowed to kiss him. In reply to her question, he had still maintained his innocence.

As the moment grew near, the crowd outside fell silent; this was broken only by a young newsboy delivering papers to the prison, who beat on the door to seek admittance. At the inquest, only a few hours after the execution, the coroner observed, 'It is a case of a moral pervert gaining lust through cruelty, is it not?'

Extract from Empire News *regarding the failure of Horner's appeal. (Author's collection)*

Doctor Shannon, the prison doctor, agreed. 'And had he escaped, he would probably have tried it again?'

'Oh, undoubtedly,' replied the doctor.

It is hardly to be denied that Charles Horner was not right in the head. He was subject to severe periods of depression after his accident, had tried to commit suicide and had assaulted his long-term girlfriend for no apparent reason. He had suddenly gone from leading a near-blameless life to being in and out of prison, and he seems to have received little or no treatment for his condition. There was no evidence brought to the court that he had ever been convicted of a sexual crime before the incident which led to his trial (although there had been the 'flashing' incident earlier on the day of the murder), so it could perhaps be said to be out of character. Much of the evidence against him was from young children, one at least of whom had demonstrated that he did not understand what he was being called upon to testify. Nevertheless, the Home Secretary felt unable to respite the death sentence.

The last previous hanging at Strangeways had been the execution of Francis Wilson Booker, on 8 April 1924. Booker, twenty-eight years old, had been convicted of the killing of fourteen-year-old Percy Sharpe, after a sexual attack in Carrs Wood, Northenden. His case was very similar to that of Horner's in many respects. Although during the First World War Booker had been awarded the Military Medal, he was also involved in petty theft and was subject to moods of depression. He had also attacked his stepmother with a knife and had assaulted a fellow employee with a hammer.

HORNER'S VIOLENT TEMPERS.

CHANGED AFTER LIFE IN THE NAVY.

By rejecting the petition of John Charles Horner (23) against the death sentence passed upon him, the Court of Appeal this week declared its agreement with the condemnation of his Judge at the lower tribunal at Manchester: "You have been found guilty of an atrocious crime."

The murder of the child, Norman Pinchen, as reconstructed by the evidence given the Court, was barbarian in its detail. But still Horner has his sympathisers. In the district in which he lived are people who admit the justice of the verdict and deny the justice of the sentence. They declare Horner to be insane. As such they contend he is entitled to the clemency of an asylum.

Flew Into Rages.

They do not base their opinion upon the condemned man's artificial attitudes in court; but upon his conduct in a more natural environment.

An *Empire News* representative is informed by a girl friend of Horner's that he is the victim of rages whose intensity is as motiveless as their occurrence.

"I have known Horner for seven years," she said, "and watched the development of this side of his character. As a boy of sixteen he was normal except perhaps that he was *too* kind for his age. One does not expect a lot of courtesy from a boy of sixteen.

"But when Horner returned from the Navy, of which he was a voluntary member, he had changed subtly. On the surface he was as usual—but he had changed.

"A first confirmation of the truth of my belief was shown at a party in the Salford district which we attended together. My escort without warning struck me. I cannot recall that I had displeased him with any remark. He just rose without warning from his seat beside me and struck me.

"I was not indignant before he was remorseful. He tried to excuse himself: he was exaggerated in his apologies. Then when I had decided to forget the incident he told me that he was suffering from severe pains in the head.

Periods of Gloom.

"It is true that when he left the Navy he was suffering from a head ailment; there was a discharge from his ear.

"I took his explanation and forgave him the blow. But weeks later the incident was repeated. As before, there was no reason in Horner's conduct. I forgave him again, for I saw that he had changed.

"Clearly, at times, he was not responsible for himself. It was not that I saw him display violence, except on the occasions mentioned, but he subjected himself to moody periods. At these times it was hopeless to try to awaken his interest.

"He was just gloomily apathetic—as he was in court when the judge sentenced him to death."

The execution has been fixed for Wednesday, August 13. It will take place at Strangeways and will be carried out by Willis.

Both Horner and Booker committed capital crimes within six years of the end of the First World War, and one may wonder whether the strains and stresses of that period had left an indelible mark on them, leading both to the gallows. At Booker's execution, questions were asked as to whether he had made a confession on the scaffold, and the same question was asked at the inquest on Horner. The Prison Governor, Major Fitzclarence, remained close-lipped. 'It is an open question whether it should be asked,' he told the inquest, 'but we are not allowed to give an answer.'

9

'WE HAVE BOTH GONE TO MOTHER'

Wigan, 1925

In the early part of the twentieth century, the only really respectable occupation for a woman was to be a housewife, and if single after the age of about twenty-six, a woman was considered to be 'on the shelf'. The sort of job open to an unmarried girl was mainly in service, which was poorly paid, often with harsh conditions and the chance that she could be dismissed at a moment's notice if she upset her employers. However, the coming of the First World War in 1914 altered all that, and as the young men rushed to join the forces in response to a massive call to arms, the government had the problem of staffing the munitions factories, running the transport networks and filling other jobs which, until now, had been a male prerogative. Conscription, which came in 1915, made matters worse. The problem was solved by relying on women, who performed surprisingly well, even in heavy industry.

One such woman was Edith Horrocks-Wilkinson, born in 1898 out of wedlock (hence the double-barrelled name), who for the first few years of her life lived with her grandparents. When she was four years old, her mother, Catherine, married Thomas Horrocks, and they lived at 55 Thicknesse Avenue, Beech Hill, Wigan, where Edith eventually joined them. Thomas was a colliery fireman, employed by Messrs Pearson and Knowles, and treated the girl as his own daughter. Edith grew up to be small, only 4ft 10in, but she made up for the lack of height with her cheery demeanour.

In 1916 she found a job in a munitions factory, where she met and grew fond of a man named James Winstanley, who she had known since the age of eleven. The romance fizzled out and Edith left the factory at the end of the war. She found a job in service, working for Mr Fry of the Black Horse Hotel, Wigan. She stayed there for three years and then had a succession of jobs as a barmaid, ending up at the Shakespeare Hotel on King Street. During this time, she met a man called Harry Taylor, and soon the two of them were often seen together in and around Wigan.

Thicknesse Avenue, Wigan, where Edith lived. (A. Hayhurst)

In 1919 Edith left home and moved in with her aunt, Ellen Taylor, at 71 Thicknesse Avenue, only eight doors away from her old address. This was mainly because she had taken to staying out late after being with Taylor, and her mother said that she was not 'having that sort of thing!' The following year she gave birth to a daughter, whom she christened Edith, and told her parents that Taylor was the father. Mr and Mrs Horrocks seemed pleased when Taylor said that he was willing to marry their daughter, but within a fortnight he had changed his mind, telling her that he did not want to be 'tied down' at this stage. He was also a little put out that Catherine Horrocks had made it quite plain to him that if he did not marry her daughter, she would not have him in her house again. However, he did promise to support the baby and for a time kept his promise.

In 1922, Taylor suddenly announced that he was emigrating to America and that when he had saved up enough, he would send Edith her passage money, so that she could come out with the child, and they would be married. For a time, Taylor kept his word and letters arrived regularly containing money for the support of his child, but in October 1924 the letters ceased.

Round about this time, Edith took up again with James Winstanley and the two seemed deeply in love. Thomas Horrocks accepted the liaison and welcomed James into his home – Edith's boyfriend even attended the wedding of Thomas' other daughter, and his father's funeral. It seemed clear to all that James was now fully accepted as one of the family.

The romance did not proceed smoothly, however. James Winstanley was a man of peculiar habits, which included a hint of sadism. He and Edith were intimate on numerous occasions and sometimes, during intercourse, James would inflict wounds on her body, such was the savagery of his lovemaking. On more than one occasion, Edith came home from a night out with James showing marks and blood flecks on her body, but she always dismissed these and made excuses for him. This led to the family taking a slightly different view of Winstanley's talents, and he found himself no longer welcome in their home.

One evening, just before Christmas 1924, Catherine Horrocks noticed Winstanley loitering outside her sister-in-law's house further along the street. The time was just after midnight and she went out and asked James what he was doing there. He said, 'I want to see Edith,' to which Catherine replied, 'Well, you are not going to see her and if you do want to see her, you must come at a decent time.'

'Edith has promised to marry me,' said James, but unimpressed, Catherine told him to go home and come again another time. At this, he went.

On another occasion in 1924, Ellen Taylor caught Winstanley outside her back door at about 11.30 p.m. one night. James was giving a whistling call and she went out to see who it was. 'What do you want at this time of night?' she asked him.

'I want Edith.' Just then, Ellen's husband came out to see what was the matter and, after a short conversation, he chased the young man off.

Although Edith had now left home, presumably for good, her mother and father continued to keep in contact. One day in February 1925, they spent a convivial evening with her at the Shakespeare Hotel, in the company of another couple, and, during conversation, Thomas Horrocks spotted a mark on the left side of his daughter's neck. It was about 2in long and rather inflamed, much like a scratch. Edith told him that her lover had done it, but nothing more was said.

On 7 March, Ernest Bennett, the landlord of the Shakespeare Hotel, was cleaning up for the night when there was a ring at the doorbell. Standing at the door was James Winstanley, and he said that he wanted Edith to go with him. Bennett said, 'Don't you think this is a ridiculous time of night to ask a girl to go out? Where do you want her to go, anyway?'

'I just want to chat with her for an hour,' James replied.

The landlord took an instant dislike to this cocky young man and told him brusquely, 'Well, she can't go out.'

Winstanley was having none if it. 'I need her to go out,' he said. 'I can't leave without her.'

Edith was, at that moment, standing on the stairs and had heard every word of the conversation. Bennett turned to her. 'Is it your wish to go with this young man?' Edith remained silent and James shouted, 'I want you to come with me.' Again, no reply from Edith. The landlord looked at her and said, 'You're not afraid to tell him "No", are you? You need not be afraid. I will see that you come to no harm.'

Turning to Winstanley, he asked, 'What is this girl to you?'

'She's all the world to me,' came the reply, 'I love her.'

Turning back to Edith, Bennett said, 'It's up to you whether you go with him or not.' For the first time Edith spoke. 'I think it is better if I go with him,' and going back upstairs, she went to her room and packed a bag, returning a few minutes later. The couple left the hotel together. She did not return to the Shakespeare until a week later and she told the landlord's wife that she had now given Winstanley up and was going to America to be with Taylor.

A few days later, Ernest Bennett went into the back kitchen of the hotel to find his wife. Edith and James Winstanley there. Edith was standing with her back to the wall and looked in a dazed condition. 'Now Edith,' he said, 'what's all the trouble here?'

'He's had hold of me by the throat and tried to throttle me,' croaked Edith. 'He told me he'd come to kill me.'

The landlord turned to James. 'What kind of a man do you call yourself getting hold of a girl and trying to strangle her?' he said, and, seizing James by the arm, threw him out. Later the same evening, he saw Winstanley loitering outside the hotel again and called the police, who moved him on.

On 16 April 1925, Edith's birthday, she received two letters in the same post. Both were from Harry Taylor and in one envelope was £10, which Harry wrote would pay for the passage of Edith and her daughter to America. There was neither apology nor any reason for the absence of letters over the last six months, but Edith now had a dilemma. She was in love with two men, but which one to choose? After much thought, she chose Harry and began to make her travel arrangements.

From letters which passed between Edith and James at the time, it appears that Winstanley was cooling off anyway and was seeking to end their relationship. However, Edith now seemed ambivalent about the situation and, despite having decided upon going to America, she wrote to James saying, 'Since we have been so much together, I would give my life for you. I cannot understand why you did not come last night. I only wish I was away from everybody, if only it was a desert, so long as I was with you.' The letter ended with a row of kisses and was signed 'Love from Edith'. In another letter, she wrote, 'I love you just the same, but if you want to finish, I will have to put up with it.'

At the beginning of May, Ellen Taylor again caught Winstanley loitering outside her house and grabbed him, saying, 'Now look here, Jim. You know that Edith has got her passage to go to America, why don't you leave her alone for the baby's sake?' James replied, 'She doesn't want to go,' and then left.

On Thursday 7 May, Winstanley received a letter addressed to him at his parent's home in Goose Green, Wigan, the house where he had lived all his life. James was not in when the letter arrived and his sister Maggie, who also lived there with her husband, took it in for him, recognising the handwriting as being from Edith. When James came in, at about 3 p.m., she handed the letter to him and he read it, before putting it into a drawer in his room. Shortly after, he got washed and went out again.

At 1.30 a.m. on the Friday morning, James arrived at the home of his brother, Thomas, who lived at Linden Avenue, Orrell. Thomas was in bed and in response to James' knocking, he staggered downstairs and opened the front door to see his brother standing there, evidently in a distressed state.

Linden Avenue, Orrell, where Winstanley was arrested. (A. Hayhurst)

'Let me in,' said James and pushed past his brother into the hall. 'I believe I've killed Edith Horrocks,' he said to a startled Thomas.

'Surely you can't have done that,' exclaimed his brother.

'I think it is done,' came the reply. 'Have you a cigarette for me?'

Thomas ushered his brother into the kitchen and gave him a cigarette. James drew on it deeply. 'I want to go home, now,' he said.

'But surely,' said Thomas, 'you'll want to go and make sure that she is really dead?'

James nodded. 'But I'm going home first.'

At 7.30 that morning James visited his brother again. 'I'm just going to have a look to see if she's gone home,' he said. Thomas stared at his brother, not knowing quite what to make of the situation. 'Let me know if she did,' he replied, and then left for work.

At teatime on Friday, James was back at home and again saw Maggie. 'Your tea's ready,' she said when he came in, but he made no reply and a few minutes later went out again. At around 11.30 p.m., he again returned home and this time saw his father, Henry, and Maggie's husband, Leonard, telling them that he had killed Edith.

'You've done a foolish thing,' said his father.

James shook hands with both of them. 'I'm going to do myself in,' he said, 'you won't see me any more. I'm going to get in front of a train.' He made for the door and as he was about to step into the street, James whispered, 'I did it at midnight on Thursday.'

A few minutes later he came in again and saw Maggie, telling her, 'I've killed my girl, Edith Horrocks.'

'Whatever have you done that for?' said Maggie.

James shook his head. 'It's done now and can't be helped. Shake hands, then I will see you no more.' Maggie shook hands and her brother left the house. 'You'll find her 400 yards up a siding near the Navigation Inn. I covered her with ferns and thorns,' were his parting remarks.

On Saturday 9 May, Thomas Winstanley was again woken in the small hours to find his brother once more on the doorstep.

'I've done it this time, I believe,' was his opening remark.

'Whatever made you do it?' said his brother.

James shrugged his shoulders in frustration. 'What could I do when she was hanging on to me like she has been doing for so long?'

'Why did you do it?' Thomas repeated.

'I'd been having a few drinks,' was the reply.

'How many drinks?'

'About fourteen,' James answered. 'She asked me to do it several times,' he added.

Thomas went into the kitchen and made two cups of tea. James sipped his, thoughtfully. 'What would you do if you were in my place?' he asked.

'If I were you I would go down to the police station and give myself up,' Thomas said.

'I will go to sleep for an hour,' spoke James, 'then I will give myself up,' and he settled back in the chair.

At 6.30 a.m. Thomas Winstanley was again woken from his slumbers. This time it was the police. Detective Inspector O'Toole and PC Cyril Ashton were standing at the door when Thomas opened it, and, after identifying themselves, they quickly went into the kitchen, where James Winstanley was still dozing in his chair.

'I've been expecting you,' he said, as the sergeant shook him by the arm. Soon, the trio were in the police car and travelling quickly towards Shevington. Suddenly, Winstanley shouted for the driver to stop. Leaving the police car, the arrested man said, 'I'll not run away, I'll show you where she is. She's dead enough. I throttled her on Thursday,' and the trio walked along the bank of the Leeds and Liverpool Canal, past the Navigation Inn (now an Indian restaurant), near the small village of Crooke.

Winstanley stopped and pointed to a clump of bushes by the side of the road, between the canal and the River Douglas. There, underneath a thin covering of ferns, was the body of a woman, lying on her back, with her head towards the canal. The body appeared to be fully clothed, although it was later discovered that she was wearing no underwear and her hair was disarranged. The mouth was open and the eyes were closed, with no signs of a struggle.

'I want to kiss her,' blurted James, but he was quickly restrained by the constable. 'See the marks on her neck where I throttled her,' he went on. 'She was always following me about and asked me many a time to do her in. She was jealous of me. I am not sorry. I would do it again. I had connections with her before I did her in. You will find her bloomers about here – she always took them off.'

The Navigation Inn – now an Indian restaurant. (A. Hayhurst)

It was near this spot that Edith Horrocks-Wilkinson died. (A. Hayhurst)

Back at the county police station, Wigan, Winstanley was searched, and £1 1s 10d in money, a metal watch, a small mirror, a black lead pencil and a Woodbine cigarette packet, which had been torn open, were the belongings taken from him. On the reverse of the packet was written in pencil, 'Good-bye to all my friends. I had to kill Edith. She asked me to. We have both gone to mother.'

On Sunday 10 May, the post-mortem was conducted by Dr George Henry Ormsby, who found that death was caused by throttling whilst the body was lying down. James was then cautioned and charged with the murder of Edith Horrocks, to which he replied, 'That is quite right. I threw her hat and gloves in the canal.'

Later, Inspector O'Toole went to Winstanley's house and found sixty-five letters, some signed 'Edith' and others signed 'Harry'. All the 'Harry' letters bore an American address. A glance at Edith's letters to Winstanley told the Inspector that for at least some of the time she was going out with him, she was head over heels in love with him.

The trial at Lancaster Assizes, commencing on Thursday 18 June, was only expected to last a single day, but it soon became obvious that it would run over, and the judge, Mr Justice Fraser, adjourned the proceedings for five minutes so that the members of the jury could contact their wives and relatives, to let them know that they would not be returning home that day. Winstanley entered the dock looking sullen and dejected, and pleaded Not Guilty to the charge of murder. Mr J.C. Jackson KC acted for the prosecution, whilst the twenty-two-year-old David Maxwell Fyfe, called to the bar only two years earlier, and at the threshold of a distinguished career as lawyer and politician, appeared for the defence. In 1934 he was to be made the youngest KC in 250 years.

Opening the case, Mr Jackson said that Winstanley had been making passionate love to Edith and they had kept company for some time, though there was a break during which another man, presently in America, intervened and became the father of her child, now five years old. He told how Harry Taylor had sent Edith money for her passage to America, but she became friendly with Winstanley again and was apparently very much in love with him, although it appeared that Winstanley's affection towards her was cooling off. Then, on 7 May, after many passionate letters had passed between them, tragedy struck and it was alleged that the prisoner had pointed out to the police where he had left the body and, when charged, admitted that he had killed her. The trial was then adjourned to the following day.

When the hearing resumed, the courtroom was packed to overflowing, the local paper reporting that a large proportion in the public gallery were well-dressed women. Dr Ormsby told the court that the dead woman had been throttled and he also commented on the marks on the dead woman's body, which he believed had been inflicted by the accused during their lovemaking. Mr Maxwell Fyfe subjected the doctor to a long sequence of questions, especially about sadism, describing it as a 'combination of acts of cruelty and desire'. Dr Ormsby said that sadism was an impulsive obsession, but qualified it by adding that it was rare in this country. He was also careful to say that in committing an act of sadism, a person knew what he was doing. The defence counsel suggested that sadism dated back to the time when men won their mates by knocking them on the head, and the doctor agreed.

The first witness for the defence was the accused, looking composed as he entered the witness box. He described his relationship with Edith, and Maxwell Fyfe asked him if she had ever complained about his treatment of her.

'Yes,' he said, 'she said that I was cruel.' At this stage, Winstanley broke down and, leaning on the rail of the witness box, he put his head on his arm and collapsed in a fit of sobbing. The judge gestured for him to be seated and then the examination continued. 'Did you know that you had done it?' asked his counsel, referring to the throttling.

'No, I did not know,' he sobbed. He then said that Edith had complained several times about his acts of cruelty, but he had known nothing about them.

'Had you got tired of this girl?' asked Maxwell Fyfe.

'No,' replied Winstanley.

'Did you still want to marry her?'

'Yes.'

Winstanley then said that Edith did not want to go to America to marry Harry Taylor, and that no matter how badly he had treated her she was determined to stick with him.

In his closing speech, Maxwell Fyfe read from some of Edith's letters, including the passage, 'There has never been a pair of lovers like us,' at which the man in the dock buried his head in his hands again and sobbed.

'The accused,' Maxwell Fyfe went on, 'enjoyed inflicting pain during sex and unwittingly carried this too far.' For the prosecution, Mr Jackson told the jury that the accused had been fully aware of what he was doing at all times, despite his claim to have no memory of the events.

The trial finished on Saturday morning – a Guilty verdict was inevitable and Winstanley was executed at Walton Gaol, Liverpool, by William Willis and Robert Wilson, at 8 a.m. on 5 August 1925. He ate a frugal breakfast, and at just before eight o'clock he asked for a drink; a single brandy was provided. Two hours later, two of Winstanley's brothers, who had cycled from Wigan, called at the prison and were allowed to see their brother's body for the last time.

10

A VILLAGE TRAGEDY

Whitworth, 1941

Lying amongst the Pennine foothills, between Bacup to the north and Rochdale to the south, is Whitworth, a town of some 7,200 souls. Whitworth is an amalgam of Healey, Broadley, Facit and Shawforth, plus several smaller hamlets linked together by the A671, part of the great eighteenth-century turnpike road. In 1941, the population was slightly more than the present day and included twenty-eight-year-old Margaret Ellen Knight, a single girl who lived with her mother and stepfather in a small stone-built cottage at 609 Market Street, Whitworth.

On Sunday, 18 May 1941, Margaret Knight was getting ready to go to the Salvation Army prayer meeting, held at 3 p.m. in the small, single-storey building that served as the meeting hall in Shawforth. She was wearing a light-coloured dress with two ruched panels down the front, fastened at the waist with a cloth belt; and she looked at herself in the mirror as she put on her new green coat with the large buttons and smoothed her precious stockings, before perching her halo hat on her head. Carefully pulling on her patent leather gloves and picking up her smart clutch handbag, she squinted at herself through her thick glasses and thought that there would be no-one smarter than her at the meeting that afternoon, then shouting 'cheerio' to her mother, she set off for the meeting.

Only one thing spoiled this idyll – Margaret Knight was pregnant. Since November 1940, she had been walking out with John Smith, a thirty-two-year-old cotton operative, who lived with his mother at 44 Back Market Street, Shawforth, about a mile and a half from Margaret's home. Smith was generally regarded as being a bit slow; he had been turned down for war service and instead had only very recently joined the local Home Guard. Their friendship had lasted a mere eight weeks, during which time Smith had often been to Margaret's house, sometimes after her mother and stepfather had gone to bed. Sexual intercourse had taken place on several occasions and, inevitably, Margaret soon found herself pregnant.

At the age of twenty-eight, Margaret Knight knew where babies came from and her immediate reaction when she found out she was pregnant was one of anger. Her boyfriend had promised to 'be careful', but had evidently not been careful enough, and whilst most girls in her position would have accepted a proposal of marriage with alacrity, Margaret, from then on, refused to have anything to do with Smith, despite him having approached her on several occasions with an offer to wed.

The first intimation that John Smith himself received that all was not well between them was one Sunday, when they had arranged to meet and his girlfriend did not appear. It was another week before he saw her again and she told him that she was pregnant and wanted nothing more to do with him. Margaret's mother, who was aware of her daughter's condition, urged her to reconsider, but without success. On one occasion, when she saw Smith in the street on a day in March, she asked him what he was going to do about it. Smith immediately said that he was willing to marry Margaret as soon as possible, but that the girl resolutely refused his offer. Agnes Holt (she had remarried) invited Smith to the house for tea and a family conference, an invitation which Smith eagerly accepted.

That evening, Smith and Mrs Holt discussed the situation together and, again, Smith repeated his offer of marriage. Meanwhile the pregnant girl sat alone in the adjoining room. Gesturing towards the door, Mrs Holt said, 'You had better go in and see what she has to say.' Doing as he was told, Smith went in and sat beside his former girlfriend.

'Is it true that you want nothing more to do with me?' he asked.

'You know it is,' retorted Margaret.

'I always tried to be careful,' Smith said ruefully, 'I never intended for you to get pregnant. I did not think it was going to happen.' The couple began to argue until Margaret stood up and faced him. 'I'll tell you what, Jack. I would rather die than marry you,' which effectively ended the conversation. Twice in the next two weeks the couple saw each other in the street, and on each occasion Smith asked her if she would come back to him, and each time Margaret refused.

The prayer meeting on Sunday 18 May was to be conducted by Mrs Alice Shorrock, who was actually John Smith's cousin, and, on entering the hall, Margaret saw her friend, Doris Crossley, a spinster who worked in one of the local cotton mills. Both girls were members of the Facit Company of the Salvation Army and were regular attenders, although neither had chosen to adopt the uniform. On this occasion, Margaret was sitting in the row immediately behind her friend, and within five minutes of the start of the meeting Doris felt a hand on her shoulder. Looking round, she saw Margaret gesturing with her hand towards the back of the hall. Lifting her head, Doris saw the figure of John Smith, wearing his Home Guard uniform, sitting at the back of the hall, his rifle resting on his knees. Smith was not officially a member of the Salvation Army, but was known to attend the occasional meeting. Quickly turning round again, Doris gave her attention to the service.

When the meeting finished, the hall emptied rapidly and Margaret and Doris walked out with Mrs Shorrock. Margaret, approximately four months pregnant, was still managing to hide her condition successfully under her coat and the three women chatted happily as they walked along. Suddenly, John Smith appeared and joined them, walking next to Margaret on the outside of the group. Doris said something to Margaret and then turned and ran back to the hall to speak to a friend. Coming out again only a short time later, she ran to catch up with her friends and noticed as she neared the group that Smith had now dropped back and was walking behind Margaret, carrying his rifle at the trail.

According to Alice Shorrock's later evidence, Smith and his former girlfriend had been arguing as they walked along, Smith saying to her, 'What have I told you about going to the Army?', to which Margaret had replied, 'That's my business, not yours.' Alice turned to Smith and said, 'What are you talking about, John? Don't be daft,' and nothing more was then said.

Doris Crossley was now within three or four yards of the group, but had paused to catch her breath. As she did so, she saw Smith lift his rifle, with the butt level with his armpit, and point the gun at Margaret. He appeared to make a swift movement with his right hand as he worked the bolt of the rifle, then there was a loud report followed by a scream, and Margaret Knight pitched forward on to her face and lay still on the pavement. John Smith immediately dropped the rifle and turned to run in the direction from which they had just come. Alice Shorrocks, stunned, ran off in the opposite direction, but after only a few paces she fell down in a dead faint.

On the other side of the street, Police Constable Henry Duncan was walking and saw the attack take place. He ran quickly to give whatever assistance he could to the fallen girl, at the same time shouting to the fleeing Smith, 'Stop! It is no use running away.' At this, Smith slid to a halt and slowly retraced his steps to where a crowd was now gathering. The policeman, with help from some of the bystanders, lifted the injured girl and carefully turned her on to her back in an attempt to make her as comfortable as possible. Blood was seeping from her mouth and an ever-spreading red stain oozed from the gaping wound in her stomach. PC Duncan thought to himself that the girl was now near death.

Another witness to the incident was Mrs Sarah Smith, John's mother. Seeing her as he came back to the scene, Smith put his arms about the deeply shocked woman and said, 'Come on, mother. It was an accident,' and the two of them slipped away through the crowd whilst the policeman's attention was diverted. Meanwhile, someone had sent for assistance and Dr Tierney arrived and pronounced the girl dead.

Smith was arrested later the same day and taken to the police station, where he was told by Inspector Ward that he would be charged with murder, to which he replied, 'I can't say 'owt. I didn't mean to kill her.' He then made a statement, as follows:

> I have asked to make this statement to make an early explanation saying what has
> led up to this trouble. [The phraseology was almost certainly that of the policeman

The murder scene. (National Archives)

The Salvation Army Hall is the single-storey building by the street lamp. (National Archives)

taking down the statement.] I started courting Margaret Knight at the back end of last year. We were very happy until a few weeks ago, when she told me she was finishing with me. This upset me very much. Some time later, I was told that she had given me up because she was afraid I would get her in the family way. I saw Margaret several times after and asked her about it, but she always gave me the same answer – 'No'. Through Margaret giving me up, I was very upset and worried about what was being said about me. On Sunday morning, I thought I would get the gun to frighten her. After dinner [meaning the mid-day meal], I went out of the house taking the gun with me. I called at the Salvation Army and she was there. On coming outside, I spoke to her and she would not speak back. After she had walked on a short distance, I fired the rifle, meaning to fire over her head, meaning just to frighten her and I was horror stricken when I saw her fall to the ground. Being so afraid, I turned and ran away. I have only been in the Home Guard about a fortnight and up to the time of me using it to frighten Margaret, I had received no instructions regarding loading and firing it and hitting her was an accident. I am very sorry for what has occurred and I did not intend to kill her [sic].

The inquest on Margaret Knight opened in Hallford Congregational School, Whitworth. On the following day, and after formal identification of the dead girl by her stepfather, Frederick Holt, the inquest was adjourned.

At the trial, conducted by Mr Justice Hallett at Manchester Assizes, on 8 July 1941, evidence was given by James Nightingale, window cleaner and also a Corporal in the Shawforth Home Guard. He said that the rifle that killed Margaret Knight was issued to Smith on Thursday 15 May and that he had given Smith a half-hour instruction in arms drill. Included in this drill was ten minutes of instruction on loading and unloading the weapon, including the working of the safety catch.

Mr Neville J. Laski, for the prosecution, turned to face the jury and asked Nightingale, 'Did he [Smith] seem wise afterwards, or was he as dumb after as before?'

'He was as dumb as before,' came the reply.

Laski went on, 'So far as you are aware, has the accused ever fired a rifle before?'

'No, Sir,' Nightingale said. He also revealed to the court that a clip of cartridges issued to members of the Home Guard would normally include five rounds, but that it would be very easy for a single round to be taken out of the clip. Cross-examined by Mr J.C. Jolly for the defence, Nightingale said that the instruction on the mechanism of the rifle, which he had given to Smith, took only a few moments.

He was followed by Leonard Ball, a Section Sergeant in the Number 3 Platoon, K Company, who for the benefit of the jury, showed them where the safety catch was and how it operated. He then inserted a single round into the Canadian Ross rifle and demonstrated how it would be forced into the breech by manipulation of the bolt, which had a straight backwards and forwards action, unlike the British Enfield 303, where the bolt had to be lifted up and then pulled back.

The murder scene as it is today. Margaret lay by the tree on the right. (A. Hayhurst)

The Company Sergeant Major of K Company told how on 17 May, Smith had returned with his rifle after an exercise and it was noticed that one round was missing from the clip that Smith handed in. When questioned, Smith replied, 'I suppose I must have lost it,' and went through his uniform pockets, but with no result. CSM Barlow pointed out to Smith that the loss of the cartridge was a serious matter and would have to be brought to the attention of the Commanding Officer, and a date was fixed for Smith to present himself and be dealt with. Since then, Smith had not appeared on any more parades and so had no reason to be wearing his uniform on the fatal Sunday, nor was he entitled to be carrying his rifle.

Mr Justice Hallett interrupted. 'Between 5.30 on the Saturday, when this round was not produced, and the afternoon of Sunday, when the fatality occurred, what opportunities had the prisoner for returning the round if he subsequently found it and wished to do so?'

'If he had found it before 7 a.m. on the Sunday, he could have returned it to Company HQ,' replied Barlow.

Next to appear was Doris Crossley, who described the events of the Sunday afternoon so far as she knew them. She had, she said, seen Smith lift the rifle and point it to the middle of her friend's back, with the butt of the rifle underneath his armpit. After firing the gun he had dropped it and ran off, whilst she ran back to the Salvation Army hall to summon assistance. When she came out again, she saw Smith returning and he said to her, 'I have done it. I didn't think there was anything in the rifle.'

When it was Smith's turn to go into the witness box, it was clear that he was going to be a difficult witness. He spoke in such a low voice that the jury complained that he could not be heard and the judge remonstrated with him on several occasions

Police photograph showing the body of Margaret Knight. The butt of the rifle can just be seen. (National Archives)

about this, telling him that it was vital for his defence that he should speak up clearly so that the jury could hear every word. Smith acknowledged this advice, but continued to give his evidence in the same low tone, to the exasperation of all in the courtroom. Smith agreed that he was responsible for Margaret's pregnancy and that he had told her and her mother that he was willing to marry the girl. At the time, he said, Mrs Holt had showed no opposition to this plan, but at a meeting at the Holts' house, Margaret had stubbornly refused to consider it.

On the day before the murder, he had been on patrol with the Home Guard and had placed a clip of five rounds of ammunition in the right hand breast pocket of his uniform. After the exercise, he discovered that one round was missing and he later found the round when he got home and took off his uniform. He decided at that time that he would take the round back to HQ the following day, Sunday. He was unable to explain his failure to find the bullet at the end of the exercise.

Questioned by counsel, he said that the contents of his uniform pocket included a pipe, a matchbox, a handkerchief and a small watch and chain. He had no explanation as to why he carried all this paraphernalia in one pocket, instead of spreading it round his other uniform pockets. When asked what he was doing with the rifle on Sunday afternoon, he claimed that he intended to take back the 'missing' round to HQ, and his only reason for going into the Salvation Army hall was to tell his mother that he might be late for their evening meal. When he saw Margaret Knight sitting in front of him, the idea came into his head that he would frighten her afterwards by firing off the round which he had in his pocket, although he meant to fire it over her head.

It was at this juncture that, once more, the judge had to caution him about the need to speak up so that everyone could hear. 'I could repeat his words to the jury,' he told the court, 'but it is a dangerous thing because I might put on a shade of voice that would alter the meaning. It is the way things are said as much as what is said.' Turning again to Smith, the judge asked, 'What you tell the jury is that when you fired the rifle, it jumped down. Is that right?'

'Yes, Sir,' muttered Smith.

'You say that the rifle – the muzzle – jumped down from somewhere above her head to somewhere about her waist as a result of the action of a single shot?'

'Yes,' Smith repeated.

'That is what you ask the jury to believe, do you?' the judge questioned.

Smith could only mutter, 'It must have been that, Sir.'

Counsel for the defence asked, 'Did you attempt to sight the rifle at all?', to which Smith replied, 'There is very little I know about a rifle.' Mr Laski then asked Smith to demonstrate how he had loaded the rifle with a single round whilst inside the Salvation Army hall, which was Smith's submission. The proceedings then almost descended into farce as Smith struggled to do as he was asked. The judge leaned towards Laski and said, 'I do not see the point of demonstrating it if he does not know how to take off the safety catch.' Neville Laski sighed and said to one of the court assistants, 'Take the safety catch off,' and then to Smith, 'Load the rifle as you did on that occasion. Show the jury all you had to do. Get the bullet out and put it in as you did.' Smith looked disconsolate as he fumbled with the bolt. 'It will not go in, Sir,' he mumbled. The judge, now as fed up with the charade as were the rest of the court, said wearily, 'Mr Laski, I doubt if this helps the jury,' and a defeated Laski sat down.

In his speech for the defence, Mr Jolly told the jury that the facts of the case were plain and simple:

It is a plain and simple case of murder. However, I submit to you that there is an alternative, members of the jury, which is open to you and it is this. It is open to you to say that he is guilty of manslaughter; because if a man, with the intention of frightening somebody, fires a rifle at another person, it is an unlawful act. If that act results in her death, it is open to the jury to say on those facts that he is guilty of manslaughter.

There is one important principle which juries are told to apply in all cases where there is a criminal case against somebody and that is that the prosecution should establish beyond reasonable doubt that the accused is guilty. It is not for Smith to prove his innocence; it is for the prosecution to prove his guilt. If you are satisfied that Smith only intended to frighten Margaret Knight, and that is the truth, there must necessarily be an end to the charge of murder. If on the other hand you are not satisfied that what the prisoner has told you is the truth, but think that it might be the truth, then it is your duty to acquit, because if you are left in that state of mind, it would mean that the prosecution had failed to discharge the burden of satisfying you beyond reasonable doubt of the prisoner's guilt.

Jolly then tried his reserve card trick, which was to get the jury to accept that Smith was mentally deficient. 'You may well think,' he said to the jury, 'that it is clear that Smith is not a very bright man. You may think it clear that he is below the average in intelligence. Of course, to fire his rifle in that way with the intention of frightening Margaret Knight was stupid and certainly wicked, but members of the jury, was it murder? May it not have been incredibly and wickedly stupid and reckless, but was it murder?'

Going over the circumstances of the shooting again, he described how the accused had passed a local policeman and other witnesses, seconds before he fired the rifle. 'If Smith had conceived the idea of killing this young woman, do you think he would have chosen a time when, if he did the act, he was absolutely ensuring, beyond a shadow of a doubt, that retribution for his crime would inevitably follow?' After asking the jury yet again to bring in a verdict of 'Not Guilty' of murder, whatever they did about a manslaughter charge, he sat down.

Prosecutor Neville Laski had little to do except reiterate to the jury that a man who deliberately loads a rifle and fires it is clearly guilty of murder if someone is killed as a result of his actions, and then it was time for the judge to sum up. He told the jury that there was no question of them regarding the killing as being justifiable or excusable. If the jury accepted the prisoner's story, that he discharged the gun only to frighten her, then the charge would be that of manslaughter, but, he said, 'The prosecution's story is that there is clear evidence which ought to lead you to the conclusion that this is not a case of manslaughter, but of murder.'

The remainder of the summing up, which was very fair and evenly balanced towards the prisoner, went on for another hour, before the judge closed:

> If at the end of it all you think that it might be true, taking the actions which the witnesses have described, this man merely intended to frighten the girl by firing over her head, why then, you ought not to find him guilty of murder. If, on the other hand, you find that his story is so fantastic that it cannot be accepted, then members of the jury, as ministers of justice, which you are, I know you will do your duty.

The jury retired at 5.20 p.m. and returned just as six o' clock was striking. The verdict was 'Guilty of Murder', although the foreman of the jury added, 'We strongly recommend him to mercy, Sir.' Donning the black cap, Mr Justice Hallett pronounced the only sentence available to him, after which Smith was taken down.

In the files of the National Archives are police photographs, one of which shows the small entrance hole of the bullet in Margaret Knight's back at about waist height, and another which shows the much larger exit wound in her stomach.

Margaret Knight lies here with her family at Facit cemetery. (A. Hayhurst)

It would have been painfully obvious to the jury that the bullet, during its passage, was aimed at Margaret Knight's unborn baby, as well as Margaret herself.

An appeal was launched on 12 July, on the grounds that the trial judge had misdirected the jury on points of law and had omitted material facts in his summing up. He had also failed to direct the jury that there was no evidence to justify them in coming to the conclusion that it was not reasonably possible for the rifle to move or kick in any direction except upwards when it was fired. These arguments found no favour with the appeal judges and a new date for the execution was set. The usual enquiry as to his mental state was made and Smith was found to be 'a hysterical type, somewhat weak in volition and liable to excessive reaction to circumstances.' He was also found to be emotionally unstable, but none of this indicated that he was insane. It was also discovered that Smith had registered himself as a member of the Salvation Army when he was taken into prison. The Army seems to have been somewhat embarrassed about this and the Governor suggested that a change of religion in the records might be more discreet, but Smith was adamant that he was a Salvationist and the designation remained. He was executed on 4 September 1941 at Strangeways Prison, by Thomas Pierrepoint.

The following reference which indicates Regn. Dist./Sub-dist./Entry No./and Month/ MUST be quoted in full in all correspondence Reference				Area of Occurrence	Area of Assignment
464	1	223	Sept	Manchester UD	32–29

Col. 1.	When and where Died.	4 Sept 1941 H.M.Prison Strangeways			
2.	Name and Surname.	John Smith		3. Sex M	4. Age 52
5.	Rank or Profession.	44 Back Market St. ~~Rochdale~~ WHITWO RTH. Cotton operative			
6.	Cause of Death.	Fracture dislocation of cervical vertebrae by Judicial Hanging Inq. F.G. Ralphs			

(6107) Wt. 25248–98 20,000 9/40 T.S. 695

Official notification stating the cause of death of John Smith. Note the pencil alteration. (By kind permission of Whitworth Heritage Museum)

Doris Crossley later married and had a family, but steadfastly refused ever to talk about the murder she had witnessed. Margaret Knight was buried at Facit Cemetery, Whitworth, in plot number 13162, belonging to her stepfather's family. She was followed twenty-two years later by her stepfather, and three years after by her mother. The grave is marked by a single small stone, simply marked 'JH', the initials of James Holt (a member of Margaret's stepfather's family), who died aged five in February 1925.

11

MURDER IN THE PARK

Southport, 1942

Victoria Park, Southport, is a site of around 34 acres, located at the south end of the town's promenade. It is a popular venue for locals and visitors alike and houses the annual Southport Flower Show, which runs for four days each year and attracts upwards of 100,000 visitors.

At around 10 a.m. on the morning of 8 February 1942, a van driver named James Rigby was taking a Sunday morning stroll in the park when something attracted his attention near the main entrance. Intrigued, he approached and found the half-naked body of a young woman lying on the grass, a few yards from the park entrance. The girl lay on her back, with her head turned to the right and with her clothing disarranged. Her dress, which was torn from top to bottom, had been pulled down to just below her breasts, thus pinning the arms tightly to her body, and underneath she was wearing a corset, from which the front suspenders had been torn. A woollen glove was on her left hand. Some distance away from the body was the other glove, two green buttons and a piece of embroidered fabric, whilst a few yards on were two pairs of women's underwear, one inside the other. On a park bench close by was a gas mask and container, plus a mackintosh. The body was cold and rigid.

Rigby immediately made for the nearest telephone box and contacted the police. Detective Constable Albert Wright and Detective Inspector Harold Mighall soon arrived, and they in turn summoned Dr Edward Cronin Lowe, Director of the Pathological Department of Southport Infirmary and Dr James Brierley Firth, Director of the Home Office Forensic Science Laboratory, Preston. The two doctors supervised the removal of the body to the mortuary, where Dr Lowe performed a post-mortem. Doctor Firth assisted in removing the remaining clothing from the body and noticed that the girl's underskirt matched the embroidered fabric that had been found in the park. The two green buttons also matched the remaining buttons on the dead girl's dress. Various bruises on the body were consistent with manual strangulation.

By 5 p.m. that day, the body had been identified as being that of Miss Imeldred Maria Osliff, who had been working as an auxiliary nurse at a nearby hospital. She was twenty-eight, unmarried and had been living with her parents in a neat little bungalow at Churchtown, Southport and travelled each day from home to work and back. She had gone to work on the morning of 7 February as usual, taking with her a handbag and a small case in which she was in the habit of keeping personal items such as letters. Her father, Frederick Osliff, told the police that his daughter had a boyfriend, Douglas Edmondson, a twenty-eight-year-old naval petty officer, of whom she had been very fond, and they had been going out together for about twelve years. When asked why the two had not married, Mr Osliff said that he was a staunch Roman Catholic and would have objected strongly to his daughter marrying outside the faith. (This mattered more in 1942 than perhaps it would in the twenty-first century and was sufficient at the time to prevent any suggestion of marriage. Imeldred would have been most unlikely to marry against her father's wishes.) However, despite her father's objections, the couple had continued to see each other.

Edmondson left school at sixteen and had then joined the Royal Navy as a stoker. At the start of the war, he was on the *Ark Royal* aircraft carrier when it was bombed for almost twenty-four hours by German planes, and had also been at Dunkirk, shortly after which he had absconded and returned to the Southport area. On 11 June 1940, he had tried to commit suicide in the pinewoods at nearby Freshfield, severing an artery in his left wrist and stabbing himself in the heart with a jack-knife. As often happens with would-be suicides, these self-inflicted wounds were insufficient to prove fatal, but Edmondson claimed to have lain unconscious in the woods for twenty-four hours. Taken to the Royal Navy sick quarters at Northern Hospital, Liverpool, his injuries were attributed to mental depression and his war experiences. Edmondson also admitted that he had stolen money from his father's house in Southport.

He then spent several months in hospital, recovering from his wounds. The following year, whilst in a fire and rescue party in Plymouth, he met with a serious accident and was hospitalised again for some time.

All the time he was away, he and Imeldred wrote to each other and Frederick Osliff handed over to the police eighteen of these letters, which he had found in his daughter's room. A few days later, two voluntary workers at the YMCA canteen in Church Street, Liverpool, noticed a bag which had been left on a table, and in it were Imeldred Osliff's handbag and a bundle of letters, which were collected later in the day by the Liverpool Police and sent on to Southport. These disclosed that Edmondson and his girlfriend had been on intimate terms for the past four years and that he had, several times, proposed marriage, and, on other occasions, suggested that they should simply live together as man and wife. It was now known that Edmondson had been seen drinking in the Zetland Hotel, Southport at 9 p.m. on 7 February; the manager, Joseph Dean, told the police that he had seen Edmondson both in the morning

Victoria Park, Southport. Imeldred Osliff's body can just be seen by the park bench on the far right. (National Archives)

and evening of that day, when he played snooker and dominoes. In the morning, Edmondson had been chatting to a friend called Ernest Taylor, and had asked him for the loan of a pound, but hearing that Taylor was now unemployed he dropped the matter. Edmondson returned later in the day and finally left the hotel at 9 p.m., saying that he had an appointment. No one had seen him since.

There was now a universal hue and cry out for Edmondson, and at 1 a.m. on 10 February PC Ernest Salt of the Birmingham Police was at New Street station with PC Wood, when they saw a man acting suspiciously. Approaching him, they asked his name and the man replied, 'It's all right. I am Edmondson,' after which he was taken into custody, where he was searched. In his pockets they found Imeldred Osliff's identity card, her clothing card and some letters. Detective Sergeant Renshaw then asked, 'How did these things come to be in your possession?' Edmondson replied, 'I took them out of Osliff's handbag. I did it.'

Later that day, Detective Inspector Mighall arrived from Southport and took Edmondson back there, where he was charged with the murder of Miss Osliff. Edmondson said that he had slept the night in Liverpool and made a statement, which said:

I met her on Saturday night at about 8.45. We had a drink in the Scarisbrick Hotel and then we went into Victoria Park where I killed her and left her. I strangled her with my hands. I took her handbag and her case because I wanted two of the letters in it. Actually there was some money in her handbag and I took that.

The neat bungalow where Imeldred lived with her parents. (A. Hayhurst)

Meanwhile, the police had been examining the various letters that had come into their possession, from which they discovered that Edmondson had married a Miss Constance Delia Chatterton, a nurse who he had first met in June 1941 at Evesham Hospital, when he had a broken ankle. At that time, Constance was engaged to a man called Sydney Minor, but this engagement was broken off shortly after she met Edmondson. The marriage took place on 16 August 1941 at Devonport, a ceremony that the bride's parents did not attend as their daughter had neglected to tell them about it. The couple then lived in lodgings for some months at 11 Collingwood Villas, Devonport, and, according to the new Mrs Edmondson, the marriage was blissfully happy, her husband still being in the navy and presumably earning a decent wage to support them both.

However, Imeldred had got wind of the proposed marriage and wrote several letters begging Edmondson not to go through with it, but once it was plain that her boyfriend had indeed married, she adopted a policy of denial, telling Edmondson that she did not believe that he was actually married to Constance, and would not until she saw their marriage certificate. She also wrote to Constance's parents along the same lines.

The matter might well have ended there; Edmondson and his new wife were safely ensconced at Devonport, well away from the aggrieved Imeldred, and he was still gainfully employed in the navy, even though his attendance record was patchy. However, it appeared that Edmondson's navy pay was not enough to cover their outgoings, and a month before the murder the couple had been in financial difficulties, which included a bill for £15 from their landlady as Edmondson had burnt a hole in the sofa, thanks to careless use of a cigarette.

In desperation, he wrote to Imeldred unashamedly asking for money. 'If only for the sake of the times we have had, will you put yourself out and try and help me. It is a desperate need and God knows how I shall get on if I can't get help.' Hardly surprisingly, Imeldred failed to come up with the money, and this is presumably why Edmondson disappeared again a week before the murder and travelled to Southport, where he stayed for a few days at his brother Norman's house. He told his brother that he was short of money and managed to borrow 10s from him on the morning of the murder, and then left, saying that he was going to Liverpool. Norman Edmondson did not see his brother again until after his arrest.

On 31 January, Edmondson called at the New Hall Annexe Hospital where Imeldred was working, and they had a conversation. A week later, Edmondson telephoned and spoke to Nurse Emily Puttick, wanting to know if Nurse Osliff was on or off duty. The nurse put him straight on to Imeldred and they again had a short conversation. At around 8.05 p.m., Edmondson telephoned again, asking to speak to Nurse Osliff. Imeldred took the call and when she finished speaking, and put the phone down, she appeared to her colleague, Assistant Nurse Rose Martin, to be somewhat annoyed. 'Prior to that,' Rose told the police, 'Imeldred had been rather depressed and had been subject to bouts of tears.' She left the Annexe at about 8.15 p.m. and the last time Rose Martin saw her, she was walking up to the entrance of Victoria Park.

The police had by now contacted Constance's family, and her mother, Nellie Chatterton, told them that there had been several letters from Imeldred Osliff to Edmondson, which she had opened and read. She had then replied to Imeldred and in return had received a telegram. Then, on Monday, 9 February 1942, at 2.15 p.m. in the afternoon, the doorbell rang at 92 Stoneleigh Road, Birchfields, Birmingham, and when Mrs Chatterton opened the door she found a man standing there who asked her to confirm her identity.

'I've got a few questions to ask you,' the man said, and was invited in. The two of them, plus Mrs Chatterton's son, went into the dining room and sat down. The man then said, 'Perhaps I'd better tell you that I am Douglas Edmondson's brother. Do you know where he and D [his pet name for Constance] are?'

'The last we heard of them, they were in Devonport,' said a bemused Mrs Chatterton. The man then said that he and his brother had been in Liverpool on Saturday night.

'Was Constance with him?' Mrs Chatterton asked.

'I've never met her,' was the reply.

Over a cup of tea there was some desultory conversation, the man saying that he was in the navy, doing clerical work. He told her that he and his brother had arranged to go and see Constance on Saturday, but that Douglas had not turned up, so he had come to Birmingham to see if he was there. Mrs Chatterton asked the man

The Scarisbrick Hotel, Lord Street, Southport, where the couple met for a drink before the murder. (A. Hayhurst)

to leave her his address but he refused, saying that he was now going back to sea; instead he scribbled his sister's address on a piece of paper and gave it to her.

He then left, but returned later at 9 p.m. and this time spoke to Mrs Chatterton's husband. 'Have you seen tonight's *Mail?*' he asked him.

'No, why do you ask?' replied Mr Chatterton.

'Because a Miss Osliff has been found strangled in Southport,' the man replied.

'What has that got to do with us,' asked the other.

'Because I definitely think my brother has got something to do with it.'

'What are you going to do?' said Mr Chatterton.

'Tell them all I know,' the other replied. 'My brother's in trouble and I'm going to help him.' He then asked the way to the police station, but, during this conversation, Mr Chatterton had been turning things over in his mind and said suddenly, 'You'll pardon me asking, but are you Douglas?'

'No,' the man replied, 'he's my kid brother.' Mr Chatterton then gave him instructions to get to Canterbury Road police station, although in the event he did not go there and was picked up at 1 a.m. the next morning and taken into custody. The man was, of course, Douglas Edmondson himself.

The trial took place in St George's Hall, Liverpool, on 20 April 1942, before Mr Justice Wrottesley. Mr Neville J. Laski KC, in his opening address, told the court that the facts of the case were very simple and very unpleasant. There could be little doubt that Imeldred Osliff had been deeply in love with Douglas Edmondson; they had been childhood sweethearts and she had allowed him to be intimate with her on frequent occasions. Despite this, Edmondson had secretly married Miss Chatterton, though his former lover had quickly found out and, not surprisingly, protested about his actions. In a letter addressed to Miss Chatterton at her mother's house, Imeldred had written:

> As I have still no word from you as regards Douglas, I thought I would write to tell you that whether you married him or not, I have still not altered my mind about him and you are only kidding yourself if you think he has forgotten me. He won't, and I think you are the most ignorant person in the world. I shall be seeing Douglas soon and will see what he has to say about the matter or the problem, shall I say, which is still unsolved but which will be solved in time.

Another letter, this one to the girl's mother, said:

> Dear Mrs Chatterton,
> Perhaps you will be interested to know that I had a letter from my young man, Douglas Edmondson, a week ago and he has still not informed me about marrying your daughter so perhaps he didn't marry her after all. Anyway, he hasn't told me so I naturally love him just the same.
> Yours, Nurse Osliff.

Mr Laski, presenting his case, suggested that the jury had a clear duty to bring in a verdict of 'Murder', and said:

> On February 7, the accused telephoned Miss Osliff and she met him in Victoria Park, where he strangled her, after which he took several letters from her case and some money. On February 9, the accused was in Birmingham and had made a rather bizarre visit to his wife's parents, representing himself to be his own brother. Perhaps he was trying to set up some sort of alibi for himself, because the Chattertons had never seen him before, but early the next day, he was spotted at Birmingham New Street railway station and there admitted his real identity. After being arrested and charged, he made a statement, which was, in fact, a confession to the murder.

Evidence was then given as to the condition of the dead girl's body and of her clothing, most of which seemed to have been ripped off in a frenzy. Doctor Firth, Director of the Home Office Forensic Science Laboratory at Preston, was asked, 'With regard to the clothing on the body, were there undoubted signs of violence, some sort of struggle?'

'I do not agree with "struggle". I found no evidence of struggle, but rather evidence the other way, although it is quite obvious to me that the girl had been subject to very considerable violence,' Dr Firth replied.

When asked if he could say how long the violence would have taken, he said, 'I should say it was fairly rapid owing to the nature of the tears. Not only the dress, but also other items of clothing were torn. I should say that they indicated tears that were done in a hurry. There was no evidence of rape,' Firth continued, 'although traces of semen were found on Edmondson's clothing and one spot on the upper part of the deceased's overcoat.' He was unable to estimate the age of the stains, nor to state definitely that they were attributable to the night of the murder.

Dr Edward Cronin Lowe was the next witness, and he described the position of Miss Osliff's body, including the presence of congealed blood on the chin and the right side of the neck. There were four separate bruises at the side of the neck and all these marks were as a result of manual strangulation. Dr Lowe said that he had then opened the body and found no evidence of any sexual violence, although he had found bruising and an effusion of blood deep in the muscles of the neck on the left side.

There then came a most important piece of evidence, the real importance of which appeared to be misunderstood by the court. The lobe of the dead woman's thyroid gland, on the left side, was actually ruptured, and it had split. 'It would not have been an easy organ to rupture, except by violent pressure,' Dr Firth said. 'The cause of death,' the witness continued, 'was due to manual strangulation, in particular the injury to the thyroid gland.'

'How did that produce death in this particular case?' asked Mr Blackledge for the prosecution.

'By the stimulation of the vagus nerve, a nerve that controls the action of the heart. The vagus nerve passes behind the thyroid gland and pressure would have to be made violently over the area of the thyroid and that would produce arrest of the heart action very suddenly,' explained Dr Firth.

For the defence, Mr Wool managed to extract from the witness that the fatal element in the strangulation was the injury just behind the thyroid gland. The judge intervened, 'Apart from that, would you have expected the deceased to have died from her injuries?'

'No,' stated the doctor.

'Do you mean to say that she would not have died from the kind of violence applied to her up to the moment she did die?'

'If it had not happened to be in that position,' was the reply.

The defence had therefore been able to show that Imeldred Osliff died solely from an accidental and incidental placing of her boyfriend's hands on her throat. If the grip had been in any other place on her neck, she might not have died. This point was not, however, taken any further.

Dr S. Barton Hall then gave evidence that he had examined the accused whilst he was in gaol awaiting trial, and considered that he was a man of unstable temperament. It appeared to him that although the accused was capable of dealing with such general stress as enemy action, he was likely to become unstable in the face of any personal stress such as financial difficulties. Extreme variations of mood in certain circumstances might involve temporary insanity.

'Would you,' asked counsel for the defence, 'say that he was a person who in extreme provocative emergency might lose the sense of right and wrong?'

'Yes,' was the answer. The court was also told that an aunt of the accused, on his father's side, had committed suicide and that another paternal aunt had been a patient in a mental hospital for two short periods.

The accused man's wife, very upset, said that she had first heard about Miss Osliff before the marriage, when she received a telegram which had been addressed to her by Nurse Osliff, at a Devonport public house. She spoke to Edmondson about it and he told her about Imeldred and just what they had been to one another. Later, she received a letter and showed it to her husband, but he did nothing about it. During their short time together they were very happy, and when her husband disappeared, on 23 January, she had no idea where he had gone. There had been no quarrel.

Then, rather curiously, Mrs Edmondson told the court that on one occasion, her husband was supposed to have made preparations for a voyage to Africa, but she subsequently found out that he had not been ordered abroad by the navy, as he had said. Another time, he told her that he had won £270 in a football competition, but when she looked into it, she found that the story was all lies. (Why Mrs Edmondson thought that evidence that her husband was in the habit of telling lies would help his case is not clear.)

It was then the accused man's turn in the witness box and the gist of his answers to counsel, and under cross-examination, was as follows:

On 12 January 1942, I went absentee. I had been taking half-days and days off and they found it out, so I lost my head and ran away. Two or three days later, I worked my way up towards Southport. I did not tell my wife I was going away, or why. I got in touch with Miss Osliff and we had tea together on 31 January at the hospital. We were not exactly friendly, but there was no argument. I saw her the next day for an hour and a half in the afternoon and I spent the next few days at my brother's house. On Saturday 7 February, I rang her up in the afternoon and I arranged to meet her at 8 p.m. at Chapel Street station. Later, I put off the meeting until 8.45 p.m. I met her at the station and she was very annoyed that I had put her off. We went together to have a drink at the Scarisbrick Arms in Southport and then walked to Victoria Park, about ten minutes' walk. It was then about quarter past nine and quite dark; I do not think that there was any moon. The conversation started off with the subject of intercourse and she suggested we should carry on those relations the same as we had before. I refused that, because I was now married and the conversation turned to money. I asked her if she could lend me any money. She asked if the money was for my own use or for this woman I was calling my wife. I said it was for both of us. She then refused to lend me any money, denied that I was married and started to become abusive about my wife, calling her a prostitute. I lost my temper then and strangled her. She would just not believe that we were married and accused us of living together unmarried. She threatened to write and tell my wife of a miscarriage she had had some years previously and that I had attempted to commit suicide two years before. I attempted no form of sexual intercourse or intimacy with her that night and I cannot explain how or why she was found half-naked. She was sitting on the park bench when I strangled her.

Shown photographs of the dead girl lying on the ground, he said he was unable to say how she got into that position. 'I can dimly remember she fell off the park bench,' he said.

He also admitted that before he went to Southport, he knew that the dead girl had communicated with his wife and her family, both before and after the marriage, and that she was more or less becoming a nuisance. Edmondson's counsel, Mr E. Wool, in his address to the jury, suggested that they might bring in a verdict of 'Manslaughter' due to provocation or, alternatively, consider a verdict of 'Not Guilty' by reason of insanity.

Judge Wrottesley, summing up, began by telling the jury that here was something which in murder trials was not often found – an account by the murderer of how he killed. He went on:

I suppose we all of us know broadly what is meant by the word 'murder'. You may take it for the purposes of this case that it means killing a human being and intending to kill him, or her. You will not need specific evidence of intention, or what is in law called malice, where a man takes a woman by the throat with both hands and chokes the life out of her. What took place here is not like a slap or blow which may chance to light on some vulnerable spot; it was taking hold of this girl, as the man who did it has told you, with both his hands and showing such violence as to rupture the thyroid gland, to bring pressure to bear on a comparatively deep-seated nerve behind and underneath the thyroid gland and so to bring about rapidly and suddenly this girl's death.

On the question of manslaughter, the judge said:

It has been said to you that you should not find him guilty of murder but may find him guilty of manslaughter because of the provocation. I am going to tell you this; that in the rather unusual facts of this case, and even if his account of what was said is true, what he told you is not sufficient to justify you saying that this was manslaughter and not murder. If the prisoner is telling the truth, the dead girl was guilty of abusing a woman she had never seen, but that abuse was not such as to justify the man taking the woman by the throat with both hands and choking the life out of her. There was nothing accidental about this killing. Both hands were used and such pressure brought to bear that the thyroid gland ruptured, and it was in that way that the nerve was pressed upon which brought her sudden collapse and death. As to a defence of insanity, two doctors were called, one for the prosecution and one for the defence, and both of them were quite unable to put before you any material that might indicate or prove that the accused was in any way insane.

The jury retired at 3.32 p.m. and returned only eighteen minutes later with a verdict of 'Guilty'. The judge then pronounced sentence of death.

A few days later, a long letter, comprising three foolscap sheets of lined paper and written in a neat hand, was sent by Edmondson to the Home Secretary, setting out his reasons for requesting a reprieve:

In no way justifying the crime of which I have found guilty [sic], I hope that the points mentioned will prove that in spite of the evidence given at my trial, many things which occurred in the past two years have had some bearing on the circumstances ... Amongst the points made was that up to January 1940, my service career had been more out-standing than average and I had been promoted to Acting Stoker Petty Officer, which rank was later confirmed and there was a possibility that I would have made commis-sioned rank in the Engineering Branch. However, I was in financial difficulty because of a sum of £15 missing from the Mess funds, for which I was responsible and though I tried to raise the money, I was unsuccessful, and that was the reason why I had tried to commit suicide ... The resulting injury to my wrist left me partially disabled and resulted in more than a year of inactivity, punctuated with long periods in hospital, including a short time in a mental ward and the Royal Naval Hospital, Gillingham. I was then put on to 'Light Duties' and remained so until April 21, 1941, when I was injured whilst fire fighting. This led to a further three months in hospital, after which there was a return to 'Light Duties'. I would submit to you that the long periods of inactivity had a very dulling effect on my mental condition and my attitude to the Service. Such a state of mind produced periods of intense mental depression ... My final point is that during the trial, both the judge and Counsel for the Crown appeared to lay great stress on the fact that I was exceedingly calm and showed no trace of mental strain during my trial. I submit that the conditions were entirely different from those on the night of the crime, when I was under great mental stress. At the time, I had heard something said of my wife that no ordinary man could hear without reacting violently in some manner. So far as the trial is concerned, I can only say that nine years of training and discipline in the Royal Navy taught me to face grave situations in a calm manner ...

An appeal on 30 April before the Lord Chief Justice, claiming that the judge mis-directed the jury in regard to manslaughter and provocation, and had failed to remind the jury that a medical witness admitted that he could not be certain that the accused must have known right from wrong at the time of the killing, failed. The execution date was set for 24 June 1942.

Shortly afterwards, the condemned man wrote to a friend, Mrs H. Cook, who kept the Brown Bear Inn in Devonport, saying, 'The appeal has failed but the result was no surprise to me. I never had any faith in it and I only gave notice of appeal to ease D's mind and let her think that I was leaving no stone unturned.'

A letter to his wife, which gives an interesting insight into the final days of a condemned man, read:

I have all the help it is possible for the authorities to give. Throughout the twenty-four hours there are two officers with me and they do all they can to keep my mind off the facts. We play cards, yarn, sing (!) and smoke for the greatest part of the day and I am tied to no real hours of going to bed and getting up. So you see, you have no cause to sit and worry about how I am passing my time. I don't want to try and think yet of the future and if we go back to the past we shall only upset ourselves, so I will say 'Goodnight'. One thing I will say is that I shall always remember our short time together because they were the finest times of all. Goodnight, my Darling and God bless you. All my love, Douglas.

The Governor of Walton Gaol received the usual reminder from the Home Office about the proceedings on the morning of the execution, including that early morning exercise for the prisoners was to carry on as usual. Prisoners normally employed near the execution shed were to be given a period of exercise in a yard remote from it, and the prison clock disconnected for the hour of the execution. At 9 a.m. on 24 June 1942, Douglas Edmondson was ushered out of this life by Thomas Pierrepoint and Herbert Morris, the drop being 7ft 11½in.

12

DEATH OF
A PAWNBROKER

Manchester, 1946

Henry Dutton (sometimes known as Harry), aged seventy-two, had a pawnbroker business at 57 Great Jackson Street, Hulme, Manchester for over thirty years. It was a depressed area, having been badly damaged during the Second World War, and Dutton's double-fronted shop now stood on its own, the properties on either side having been demolished during the air raids. The elderly pawnbroker was now struggling to make a living, and, to make matters worse, he had suffered several burglaries during the past eighteen months.

Inside, the shop (which was partitioned off from the rest of the premises) was roughly 11ft by 9ft. Clothes lay scattered around, including a gent's raincoat and a poor quality suit, waiting for payday so that their owners could come and reclaim them. A row of books stood on a shelf at the end of the shop and in a glass showcase, set well out of reach of customers, were rings and watches, the only things in the shop that had any real value.

On Monday, 26 November 1945, a lorry driver, Harry Dixon, was driving his vehicle along Great Jackson Street when he saw what he described as an 'old gentleman', wearing a brown overall coat, staggering out of the shop. It looked to Dixon as though the 'gentleman' was trying to attract his attention, so he pulled in to the side of the road. The man was Harry Dutton, who took another few faltering steps before collapsing onto the pavement, so Dixon got down from his lorry to give assistance. Looking round, he noticed that there appeared to be blood on the front step of the shop and waved to his assistant, Frank Laverty, telling him to find a policeman as quickly as possible, whilst he stayed to comfort the injured man.

It was just after 2.30 p.m. when PC Frederick Magerkorth, of the Manchester City Police, received instructions to go to Great Jackson Street, where he found Harry Dutton bleeding from wounds in the lower part of the stomach and the right thigh. Rendering what first aid he could, and making Dutton as comfortable as possible, he

The bomb-damaged pawnbroker's shop. (National Archives)

left the old man with the lorry driver and had a quick look round inside the shop, where he found two empty cartridge cases just inside the entrance. Later, he accompanied the injured man to Manchester Royal Infirmary, and, whilst Dutton was being removed from the ambulance, Magerkorth noticed a bullet on the stretcher which Dixon had just been lying and quickly picked it up. Three days later, one of the nurses on Dutton's ward found another bullet in his bed, which she handed to the police.

The shop premises and surroundings were searched thoroughly by the police, and on the pavement outside they found several bloodstains. Inside the shop, the counter, which was about 3ft high, bore the mark of a bullet hole 27in from the floor. In a drawer immediately behind the counter, Detective Chief Inspector Frank Stainton found a bullet embedded in the drawer bottom, and, on the floor at the end of the counter, he also found an empty cartridge case. Later in the day, Albert Allen, a member of the staff at the Home Office Forensic Science Laboratory in Preston, visited the shop and took certain measurements. It was of his opinion that the bullet which had been found lodged in the drawer had been fired from hip height, and fired from against the entrance wall, just inside the door of the shop.

The shooting had actually been witnessed by ten-year-old Jimmy Davies, who had been hanging around the shop doorway with some of his pals, when suddenly they heard what sounded to them like two shots coming from inside the shop. Most of the lads ran away, but Jimmy was made of sterner stuff and, keen to find out what was going on, stood his ground. He saw a man walk slowly out of the shop, look up and down the street and then take to his heels. Seconds later, the man all the local boys knew as 'Uncle Harry' came staggering out and fell on to the pavement. Jimmy then decided that discretion was the better part of valour and headed for home, where he blurted out his story to his parents, who promptly took him down to the police station. Young Jimmy was able to give the police a good description of the man: about twenty-five years old, 5ft 7in in height, dark hair and clean-shaven. 'The man,' said the boy, 'wore sailor's bell bottom trousers, a seaman's blue jersey, light brown jacket and black shoes. He had no hat on and his hair was black and curly in the front.' This information was to lead to one of Manchester's greatest manhunts.

Back at the hospital, the gravely ill Harry Dutton was also able to give a rough description of his attacker, which matched that given by the young witness, although Dutton insisted that the man who shot him was wearing a brown trilby. Dutton had a bullet-entry wound in the right-lower part of the abdomen, with a corresponding exit wound in the right buttock. There was a second entry wound in the right upper thigh, with a corresponding exit wound at the back of the same thigh. He was suffering from extreme shock, for which he was given a plasma transfusion, and, at 5.15 p.m. that day, Dutton was operated on and it was found that a bullet had passed through the right side of the abdomen and the large bowel, creating severe injuries. Even so, the old man was well enough to receive a visit from his son, Thomas Dutton, a Bank Manager. Meanwhile, the police were vigorously pursuing their enquiries and the headline in the *Manchester Evening Chronicle* on 27 November read, 'Shot Pawnbroker: An Arrest Expected'.

The *Chronicle* said that the pawnbroker was still very ill and there followed a description of the man that Dutton had given to the police. It went on to mention a raid by three men on a Manchester jeweller's shop a few days previously, when a tray of valuable rings had been stolen after the shop window was smashed. The men had got away in a stolen car, which was later found abandoned near London Road station, and the jewellery in the shop window had been so widely scattered by the thieves that it had proved impossible to discover, to date, exactly how much was missing. The police were keeping an open mind as to whether the two incidents were linked, and, because of this, some confusion arose in the early stages of the investigation. However, in the end, it was found that they were not linked.

That same day, a man named William Phelan was in the Salvation Army Hostel in Francis Street, Manchester, when he fell into conversation with a man named Martin Patrick Coffey, who he knew slightly having seen him in the hostel before. During the conversation, Coffey suddenly announced that he had shot a man and, when questioned, said that it was a pawnbroker in Jackson Street, the day before. Phelan waved a hand at him. 'Rubbish,' he said, 'I don't believe you.'

Just then, they were joined by a man named John Irvine, who was carrying a copy of the *Manchester Evening Chronicle*, from which he began reading snippets out to his companions. As he read the paragraph concerning the shooting at Harry Dutton's shop, he noticed that Coffey appeared to be laughing, and when he asked the man why, he replied, 'I am laughing up my sleeve at the description in the paper. It was me that done the job.'

The other two looked at him. 'You're joking,' Irvine said and Phelan sat there with a disbelieving look on his face, saying nothing. Coffey continued:

Straight up. The job was done on Monday at two o'clock. I went into the shop and asked the old man if I could have a look at an overcoat that was hanging up. He took the over-coat down and put it on the counter for me to look at. I then pulled out a gun as the old man made to go round the back of the counter. I told him to hand over all the money that was under the counter and he put two or three thousand pounds on the counter.

At this, Irvine's eyes widened, 'How much?' he uttered.

'Two or three thousand,' repeated Coffey and went on, 'I asked him to put the rest of the cash on the counter and as he was fumbling to pull out some more money, a gun suddenly appeared in his hand. I shot the gun from his hand and wounded him on the wrist. He then pulled a whistle out of his pocket and blew it two or three times. I fired two or three rounds into his stomach and the old man staggered after me as I legged it from the shop.' (These words were taken from statements which the men later gave to the police.)

By now, Irvine was all agog. He asked, 'What did you do with the gun?' But his friend ignored the question and simply said, 'I got on a bus and went home.'

'But the paper says that there were two men,' persisted Irvine.

'No, I was on my own,' replied Coffey.

Still having difficulty in believing what he was being told, Irvine questioned, 'Why did you do it?' and the reply was, 'No reason at all. I did it on the spur of the moment.'

Later, the three men were walking up Market Street and Coffey left the others for a few minutes, darting into the ruins of a bombed-out house. Coming back, he showed them a handkerchief, in which was wrapped a gun. He handed it to Irvine and said, 'Be careful, it's loaded.'

'I'll keep this in case you get into any more trouble,' said Irvine, putting the gun into his coat pocket. He had hardly done this when the three men were confronted by a police constable, who arrested Coffey on a charge unconnected with the shoot-ing and took him to the nearby police station. The other two men split up, but met again later in the day at Irvine's lodgings, where Irvine removed all the bullets from the gun and placed it on the top of his wardrobe. Irvine was also in possession of Coffey's trilby hat, which he said he had picked up from a table at the hostel, where Coffey had put it down.

At 5.30 p.m. that day, Coffey was interviewed by Inspector Frank Stainton at Bootle Street police station and told, 'You answer the description of a man who was seen in the vicinity of a pawnbroker's shop in Great Jackson Street yesterday afternoon about the time that the pawnbroker was shot whilst carrying on his business there.'

Asked to account for his movements between 2 p.m. and 3 p.m. on that day, Coffey replied:

That's easy. I wasn't in Great Jackson Street and I haven't shot anybody. I stayed at the Salvation Army in Francis Street on Sunday night and occupied bed 290. I left the Army on Monday morning at half past eleven. I went to London Road Station and hung around there till one o'clock, then I went to the amusement arcade in Deansgate, and from there back to the Salvation Army for my dinner, where I stayed until half past 2. From there, I went up Cheetham Hill Road.

Inspector Stainton indicated to Coffey that he was far from satisfied with his story and Coffey was locked up pending further enquiries.

At closing time, 3 p.m., on Friday 30 November, in the Robin Hood Hotel, the barmaid called 'time' and went on collecting glasses. Glancing round, she saw that there were three men left in the bar and she shepherded them to the door and pushed them out into the street. Coming back into the pub, she spotted a man who she usually called 'the little fellow' (John Irvine) lying under a low bench that ran round the bar. Although Irvine protested that he was only hiding out of the way to 'get a little kip in the warm', the barmaid suspected that he had other motives and called the police.

'You coppers don't want to waste your time nabbing fellers like me,' he blurted out when the police arrived. 'I can put you on to a real criminal.' Soon he was telling his story to Inspector Stainton, who then accompanied him to his lodgings at 3 George Street, Old Trafford, where Stainton found the pistol and bullets and took possession of them.

By now, the unfortunate Harry Dutton had died and Stainton told Coffey that the charge against him was now murder and that the police were holding an automatic pistol, which they thought was his. Coffey immediately owned up and said, 'You're right. That's my pistol. I did it. I would have told you before but I was frightened that the old man would die. Now that it doesn't matter, I will tell you the truth.'

He then dictated a statement and signed it, and in reply to Inspector Stainton's charge that he 'did feloniously murder one Harry Dutton on the 26 November 1945' (not strictly correct because Dutton did not die until the 30th), Coffey replied, 'Nothing to say.' He was charged at Manchester City Police Court on 1 December, the hearing lasting only three minutes and the accused man being remanded in custody. At a further hearing, on 19 December, he was remanded to the next Manchester Assizes.

There, Mr Justice Morris listened patiently to the police and other witnesses, Coffey choosing to remain silent. Detective Sergeant Arthur Ormston gave evidence that he knew Coffey well and had seen him dressed in sailor's clothes, as described by young Jimmy Davies. Alice McKittrich, a bystander, said that she remembered being at the corner of Great Jackson Street on the day of the crime and had seen Mr Dutton outside his shop, playing with a little white dog. Later, she had seen a man come out of the shop wearing sailor's trousers, a short coat and a trilby. However, she had attended an identity parade on 5 December and had failed to pick anyone out.

Firearms expert Albert Louis Allen said that the gun produced in court was a self-loading 7.65mm pistol, in good working order, and that Harry Dutton's clothing bore several holes all consistent with holes caused by 7.65mm bullets. Tests on Dutton's brown overall indicated that the shots must have been fired at a range of more than 9in, as evidenced by the absence of scorch or powder marks on the material.

'It is not a true automatic weapon,' the expert said. 'It is necessary for a separate press on the trigger for each shot to be fired.' The trigger pressure was 11lbs, heavy for a weapon of that type, and in his opinion, the cartridge cases produced in court had been fired from that gun.

Counsel for the defence, Kenneth Burke, tried to make out that his client had fabricated the story he told to Phelan and Irvine. 'There was no evidence that Harry Dutton had the sort of money my client later talked about. Neither has any evidence been produced of the deceased pawnbroker ever having had a pistol. It was sheer romancing on his part, as was the rest of his story,' Burke said.

Burke had perforce to admit that, as the defendant had given a signed confession to the police, his task was a difficult one, but he urged the jury to give importance to Coffey's replies when first confronted by Inspector Stainton. At this time he had immediately denied that he had shot Dutton, or anyone else, and had given a coherent account of his movements at the critical time. Burke did not mention though that he had not been able to bring any witnesses to support his statements.

'Coffey,' Burke told the court, 'was vainglorious and had said certain things in order to be in some sort of limelight. Had he kept his mouth shut, there would have been no case against him.'

The judge told the jury that the law presumes malice if there is a deliberate act of a cruel nature, such as a shooting, but that if they had any reasonable doubt as to the facts, they should acquit. Despite this, no one in the courtroom had any doubt what the jury's verdict would be and, forty-five minutes later, the death sentence was passed on Coffey, who smiled and was then taken down.

An appeal in front of the Lord Chief Justice failed and Lord Goddard of Aldbourne said dismissively:

This is another of those cases in which the prisoner, being convicted of murder on the clearest possible evidence, for the sake of getting the sentence postponed for a time, appeals and puts forward no grounds at all for the appeal. It is suggested in this case that the learned Judge (Morris) should have directed the jury to manslaughter. The prisoner shot him, I may say, like a dog!

Whilst in Strangeways Prison, on the eve of his execution, Coffey wrote to his father:

When you get this, everything will be over, so make up your mind to forget me ... I am not afraid so don't worry about me and look after yourself. You gave me good advice often enough and I would not take it. No one is to blame only myself – I done this crime and I have to pay for it. I had a fair trial and I lost, so I can't kick ... from your ever loving and foolish son.

P.S. I am sorry for bringing my family a bad name. My last wish is that you try and forget me.

A letter from his brother, Michael, to the Home Secretary, written ten days before the execution, said, 'I once again take the liberty of writing to you to make a final appeal for my brother Martin P. Coffey.' He mentioned that the convicted man had a medical complaint and had been told that he had only twelve months to live. 'I would like you to take into consideration the effect it will have on anybody's mind to be told they only had six months or a year to live with his complaint. It is likely to unbalance the most normal person and his mind is definitely not normal,' he pleaded.

The letter made no difference and on 24 April 1946, at nine o'clock, Thomas W. Pierrepoint and his assistant, Alexander Riley, ended the argument for good.

13

'IN ONE OF
MY FUNNY MOODS'

Rawtenstall, 1948

The town of Rawtenstall, in the south-east corner of Lancashire, lies in the Rossendale valley on the edge of the Pennine moors, drained by the River Irwell as it trickles its sluggish way through Bury and Manchester. The origin of the name is lost in time, although it is thought that it referred to buildings occupied when cattle were pastured on the high ground. It had once been a thriving town, thanks to the Industrial Revolution and the cotton trade, but by 1948 the mills were beginning to fall silent and the population, 30,000 in the 1911 census, had declined to 27,000. The streets were mostly terraced houses running down to the valley bottom, along which ran the A681, Bacup Road, paved in stone setts with the occasional scattering of tarmac.

Number 137 Bacup Road was a curious stone-built cottage, which stood back-to-back with the eighteenth-century three-storey 'Weavers' Cottage', immediately behind it, now in the care of the Rossendale Civic Trust. It stood on the corner of Bacup Road and Fall Barn Fold (or Close), a narrow thoroughfare that ran over the culverted River Irwell, leading to a level crossing on the Bacup branch of the London, Midland and Scottish railway. Overhanging the river was a signal box, and the line itself could be crossed by a rickety footbridge. The Irwell, normally a sluggish and heavily polluted stream, flowed over a weir, several yards back from the culvert, which created a head of water several feet high. In times of heavy rainfall, the amount of water flowing over the weir could be quite substantial, but normally the river at this point was quite shallow.

The small house, fronting on to Bacup Road, was occupied by forty-one-year-old Margaret Allen, the twentieth child of twenty-two siblings. She had lived with her mother until her mother's death, in January 1943, and had moved into No. 137 that year on her own, having very few friends. The street door opened on to a small scullery on the left, which was fitted with a stone sink, and to the right was a coal

Number 137 Bacup Road, Rawtenstall. (National Archives)

Contemporary picture showing Fall Barn Close. The River Irwell flows immediately behind the signal box. (By kind permission of Rossendale Civic Trust)

place, merely a brick-lined cubbyhole. Another door led to the only proper down-stairs room, approximately 18ft by 14ft, with some stone steps on the left, which led upstairs to the single bedroom. The few people who found their way into this dwelling found it dirty and very sparsely furnished, with just one balloon-back chair and a makeshift table, covered with a rough cloth. The floor was covered with old linoleum, the pattern on which had largely worn away.

The view from Margaret's front door looked across Bacup Road and over the ground used by the Rawtenstall Cricket Club, to the right of which was a row of semi-detached houses of considerably better quality than the virtual hovel she occupied. In common with many working class girls in Lancashire, Margaret had received a rudimentary education until she reached twelve, when she went as a 'half timer' in the local mill, a scheme that permitted children to split their time between the mill and the schoolroom. At age fourteen, she began working full time in the mill and later had a number of other jobs, including temporary post woman and bus conduc-tress, interspersed with time off due to ill health. A final spell as a slipper operative in a local mill ended in January 1948, from which time she was unemployed again, due to ill health.

For a number of years it had been Margaret Allen's custom to wear men's cloth-ing, and these days, she would be described as a crossdresser, although such a word would have been foreign to the folk of Rawtenstall in 1948. She insisted on being called 'Bill' by her workmates, although she indignantly denied any abnormal sexual tendencies, and she admitted to having the occasional boyfriend, although these friendships did not usually last long. Her time on the buses was probably one of the happiest interludes of her life, as most of the 'clippies' wore slacks, rather than a skirt. However, this gave rise to a certain amount of difficulty with her colleagues; some of the male drivers refused to work with female conductors. Her best (and pos-sibly only) friend by 1948 was Annie Cook, who she met every Saturday morning to

The Ashworth Arms,
where Margaret and Annie
used to go after shopping.
(A. Hayhurst)

go shopping, and it was their habit to call in the Ashworth Arms on Burnley Road afterwards to have a chat over a drink.

One day, Margaret confided in Annie that she had had an operation for a sex change at St Mary's Hospital, Manchester, although whether this was true was never ascertained. Last Whitsun, she and Annie had gone to stay for a few days' holiday with a Mrs Wheeler, who kept a boarding house at 92–94 Talbot Road, Blackpool. Margaret had registered herself as 'Mr Allen' and Annie as 'Mrs Allen', although Annie said later that she had not been comfortable about that. A photograph of the couple taken at the time shows the two of them looking neatly dressed, with 'Bill' sporting a slicked-down hairstyle and a man's shirt and tie.

She was now living on 11s a week public assistance and 26s a week National Health sick pay, and, hardly surprisingly, she was in debt to the tune of £46, a considerable sum at this time. Her rent of 6s 4d per week was in arrears by £15, plus bills for electricity, coal, logs and more, which had accrued since November 1946. There had also been several County Court judgements registered against her, and in August 1947 she had been fined 40s for larceny. If it bothered her she never showed it, but she must have realised that she had little or no chance of clearing her debts, and the landlord was beginning to make noises about her arrears, so she faced being thrown out on to the street. In addition, despite her longing to be a man, she was going through the menopause and often needed to sit down due to dizzy spells.

At the beginning of August 1948, Margaret made the acquaintance of Mrs Nancy Ellen Chadwick, who was employed as housekeeper to a Mr Whittaker of Hardman Avenue, about half a mile from Margaret's home. Mrs Chadwick had the reputation of being a fussy, eccentric old biddy, who wore Victorian clothes and often had on odd shoes and stockings. She was also said to be something of a fortune teller with a talent for reading tea leaves. It was common gossip in the town that Mrs Chadwick had lots of money and was suspected of carrying it round with her.

The two had first met at the house of a Mrs Haworth and they met again a week later in the centre of the town. During conversation, Mrs Chadwick mentioned that she had just run out of sugar and Margaret offered to bring her a cupful. Such commodities were still on ration after the war and Margaret's gesture would have been considered very generous. However, although she visited Mrs Chadwick's home on a regular basis after that, somehow the promised sugar never materialised. On Saturday 21 August, at 8.30 a.m., Margaret made yet another visit to Nancy Chadwick's and, again, mentioned the possibility of her having sugar available on the following Monday.

Margaret Allen. (Author's collection)

However, Nancy Chadwick was getting more and more curious about the little woman in men's clothing and later on that morning, at about nine thirty, she appeared walking down Bacup Road and was just outside No.137 when Margaret Allen came out, intending to do some shopping. Whether this meeting was engineered by accident or by design is not clear, but immediately Nancy struck up a conversation and made it plain that she expected to be invited inside the house, a suggestion that Margaret hastily rejected.

'I'm afraid I haven't got time now, Nancy,' she said, 'you can see inside another time.' But she found herself being pushed back into the scullery as Nancy Chadwick made a determined effort to gain entrance. Margaret still protested, but Nancy now had the bit between her teeth and was shutting the front door behind her and making for the living room.

That evening, the local bus employees were holding an important union meeting, which actually went on until well into Sunday morning. Herbert Beaumont, a driver for the bus company, agreed to take some of the members home on his bus, almost certainly in direct contravention of his employers' rules, and he left the garage with his load of passengers at about 3.55 a.m. Driving his number 46 bus along Bacup Road, with all his lights on (what street lights there were had been switched off for the night), he saw what looked like a bundle of rags on the road in front of him, and, stopping to examine it, discovered that it was the body of an elderly woman lying face downwards. The body was lying at the junction of Bacup Road and Fall Barn Fold, with the head completely covered with a coat. In the light of his headlamps Beaumont could see that the figure was wearing stockings and socks, with shoes.

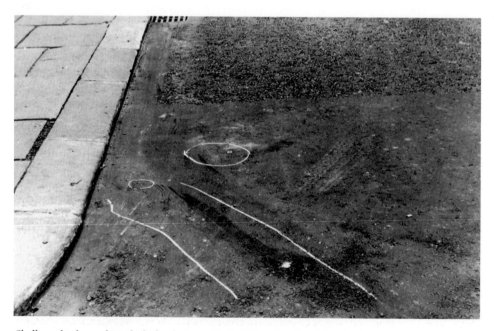

Chalk marks show where the body of Nancy Chadwick lay. (National Archives)

Beaumont stayed at the scene whilst one of his passengers, Joseph Unsworth, raced back to the depot and hurriedly phoned the police. The call was taken by PC Stanley Marsden, who soon appeared at the scene and noticed that the dead woman lay with her head resting on her forearm. Telling one of the busmen to fetch a doctor, Marsden began, painstakingly, to mark the outline of the body on the road with a piece of chalk. She was lying with her head about a foot from the kerb, with her feet extending towards the middle of the road, almost exactly outside Margaret Allen's front door.

Dr Frederick Percival Kay arrived and stated that the woman was dead, expressing the opinion that she had been dead about ten hours. The body was cold and rigor mortis was setting in. There was a deep laceration on the top of her head, her hair was matted with blood and her face appeared to be dirtied by a covering of fine ashes. There was also blood on her hands and forearms.

Dr Kay told the constable that the injuries were not consistent with the woman having been knocked down by a motor vehicle, and, taking hold of the woman's right arm to turn her over, he found that the arm was very stiff. 'Anybody know if this woman was a cripple?' he asked the little knot of men gathered round. No one did. With the assistance of one of the busmen, the doctor then had the body removed to the other side of the road and waited for more police to arrive.

In the dim light of his police lamp, Constable Marsden noticed a patch of blood where the woman's head had been and a semi-circular drag mark from the body to the kerb in front of No.137, measuring 27ft and about 1ft 3in wide. The policeman made a note in his book that he had patrolled Bacup Road in the beat car at 3.30 a.m. that morning and there had been no body in the roadway at that time.

Police photo of the scene. Note Nancy Chadwick's covered-up body on the right-hand pavement. (National Archives)

Two bus men, who had elected to walk home from the union meeting, later told the police that they had passed the spot at 3.45 a.m. and had noticed nothing, which meant that the body must have been placed on the road between 3.45 and approximately 4 a.m.

Detective Constable Harold Rowbottom of the Preston Forensic Laboratory arrived at about 9 a.m. and proceeded to take samples of the debris on the road and of the fire-ash that had apparently fallen from the body. Later that morning, Dr Gilbert Bailey conducted a post-mortem and Mrs Chadwick's nephew, William Barnes, identified the body. Dr Bailey found that the vault of the skull was fractured in several directions over almost the whole of the skull, and there were seven incised wounds to the head, each just over 1in long. The cause of death was shock, produced by multiple fractures to the skull and haemorrhaging of the scalp wounds. It was apparent that Nancy Chadwick had suffered a frenzied attack with a heavy implement.

News of the murder soon spread and many people gathered on Bacup Road to watch the police as they searched for clues. Several people said that they had seen Nancy Chadwick on the day she died, Bertha McGarrigan saying that she had seen her in Woolworths at 2 p.m. The signalman at the Fall Barn crossing, Robert Murphie, told the police that he had seen her, at 5.30 p.m., going towards Bacup Road. Other sightings were at 8.20 p.m. by Arthur Wogden, who saw her in Bury Road, and Emily Whittaker was sure she had seen her at 10.30 p.m. in Fall Barn Fold, in company with a man. All these sightings were to prove false.

Sometime during the morning, Margaret Allen approached the police and offered to view the body to see 'whether it was identical to that of a woman named Chadwick who lived with that old chap Whittaker.' This offer was accepted and she went to the mortuary and saw the body. After looking at it for a few minutes, she said, 'I'm not quite sure about the face because her mouth is puckered up, but that is the same coat she had on yesterday. Can I open the mouth? She has two fangs top and bottom and I could tell with them.' The police hastily declined this offer.

On 29 August, at 2.30 p.m., some ten hours after the discovery of the body, Margaret Allen, together with two locals, Mrs Gertrude Caine and Jack Ives, walked up the Fold leading to the River Irwell and the railway line. The area was full of police officers and as the three neared the river, Margaret gestured at something in the water, and minutes later she pointed it out to Detective Constable Joseph Blinston saying, 'There's a bag in the water. Look, it's there.' The officer scrambled down the bank and managed to retrieve what turned out to be a string bag, inside which was a ladies' handbag.

For the next few hours, Margaret Allen wandered along the river bank as the police officers continued their search and, although she made no attempt to help or to impede their progress, the officers were aware of her presence and it was the subject of some jocular remarks between them. Meanwhile, the local paper carried the headline, 'Widow murdered for money, theory'. It went on to say, 'Mrs Chadwick, a widow, was usually shabbily dressed and to a stranger would appear to be a poor

The shallow water below the weir, where police found Nancy's bag. (A. Hayhurst)

person. Actually, she owned four houses left her by a former employer ... A number of objects, including a spanner, were removed by the police today from a works yard off the Rawtenstall- Bacup road.

Later that afternoon, police searchers found fresh bicycle tyre marks on the narrow path running along the bank of the Irwell, near the spot where the handbag had been found. Photographers and forensic science experts were rushed to the spot and photographs were taken of the tyre marks, whilst plaster casts were taken of two pieces of iron strip found nearby. The newspaper reported that the path was scarcely ever used nowadays, according to local residents.

The police were now starting a house-to-house search of the area, under the watchful eye of Chief Inspector Bob Stevens of Scotland Yard, who had been called in to assist, together with Chief Superintendent John Woodmansey of Lancashire CID. Margaret Allen was seen at the police station and made a statement to the effect that she had known the dead woman for about a month and had visited her several times. She mentioned the cup of sugar that she was hoping to get for Mrs Chadwick and the fact that the woman had appeared outside her house and had asked to be admitted. She had refused to let her in, she said, and told the police that Mrs Chadwick had never been right inside her house, only just inside the front door. Mrs Chadwick had then gone away and that was the last time that Margaret had seen her. She had heard nothing during the night and was awoken the next morning by the police knocking on her door. The police then accompanied Margaret back to her house and carried out an inspection, paying particular interest to the fire grate. Then, thanking her for her co-operation, they left.

The next morning, the police reappeared and Allen was again taken to the police station, where she made an amended statement, altering minor details but not the main part of her story. She again stated that she had stayed in all night on the Saturday and never went out between ten o'clock and eleven the next morning.

At noon, Chief Inspector Stevens and Chief Superintendent Woodmansey accompanied Allen to her house, and, just inside the coal place, found three large bloodstains, which appeared to have been missed the day before. Woodmansey called for Allen to go into the coal place and showed her the stains, asking her for an explanation, to which she made no reply. Chief Inspector Stevens then asked the same question and, again, Margaret stayed silent. The three then returned to the

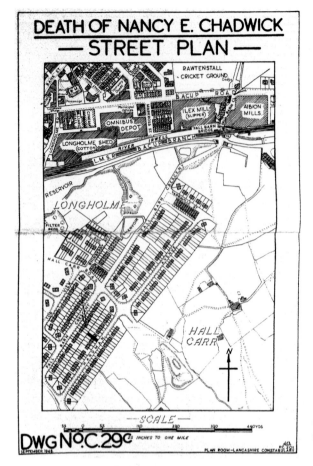

Street plan showing the area around 137 Bacup Road. (National Archives)

living room, where they saw a shopping bag and Stevens said to Allen, 'This bag contains ashes and three pieces of rag.' Taking the items out of the bag, he held up a piece of maroon-coloured cloth. 'This piece is wet,' he said. 'Everything else is dry. What have you used this cloth for?'

'That's a floor cloth,' was the reply.

Stevens held up the cloth again. 'It's quite wet. When did you use it?'

Margaret Allen made no reply, but walked over to the sofa and picked up her mackintosh, which had been lying on it. 'Come on,' she said quietly, 'I'll tell you all about it.' Chief Inspector Stevens then cautioned her and she said, 'Let's get out of here.'

Passing the coal place on the way out, she gestured towards it and said, 'That's where I put her.' The forensic report later showed that a hair found in the ashes was identical to one taken from the head of the deceased, and also amongst the ashes were two small pieces of metal which could possibly have come from the clasp of Nancy Chadwick's handbag.

Back at the police station, Margaret Allen asked to make a third statement. 'The other statements I gave you were wrong,' she said, before delivering her third:

As I was saying, I was coming out of the house on Saturday last about twenty past nine in the morning, when Mrs Chadwick came round the corner. She asked if this was where I lived and could she come in. I told her I was going out. I was in a funny mood and she seemed to get on my nerves, although she hadn't said anything. I said I would have to go, as I was going out and she could see me sometime else, but she seemed somehow to insist on coming in.

I just looked round and saw a hammer in the kitchen. This time we were talking just inside the kitchen with the front door closed. On the spur of the moment, I hit her with the hammer. She gave a shout that seemed to start me off more. I hit her a few times but I don't know how many. I then pulled the body into my coalhouse. I've told you where I was all day, that part is true and true that I went to bed at ten to eleven. When I awoke, the thought of what was downstairs made me keep awake. I went downstairs but couldn't tell the time as all the clocks are broke [sic]. There were no lights in the road and I couldn't hear any footsteps. My intention was to pull her into the river and dispose of the body but she was too heavy and I just put the body in the road. Later, I heard the noise outside and knew they had found her. I looked out of the window and saw the bus. Then I went back to sleep. Just before I put the body out, I went round the corner and threw the bag in the river. The bag I sort of dropped in, the hammer head I hit her with I threw some distance up the river and the handle I used for the fire. I looked in the bag but there was no money in it. I didn't actually kill her for that. I had one of my funny turns. The bag you found this morning has the ashes from the coalhouse. They were there when I put the body in, as was an antimacassar I burnt on the Sunday. I had no reason to do it at all. It seemed to come over me. The noise after the first hit seemed to set me off.

A later search with army metal detectors failed to find the hammer-head murder weapon.

At the trial, before Mr Justice Sellers at Manchester Assizes, no attempt was made by the defence to deny that the deceased woman had met her death at the hands of the prisoner, but the defence sought to obtain a verdict of 'Guilty but Insane'. Defence counsel, Mr Gorman, did not put Allen in the witness box, but he stressed the entire lack of motive and pointed out that there was no evidence that the murder had been committed for gain. The accused woman had a history of 'funny turns' and suffered from headaches. He called Annie Cook, who testified that she had, on one occasion, told Allen to pull herself together and eat properly, upon which the accused had rushed over to the gas tap and turned the gas on, putting the gas tube into her mouth and shouting, 'You are trying to break up a friendship.'

Mr Whittaker, with whom the deceased woman had lived, testified that during the week preceding the murder, he had seen Mrs Chadwick transferring money to a new purse, which a nephew had bought for her, and estimated that there was two or three pounds in it.

The prison Medical Officer said that there was no evidence that the accused suffered from any serious physical or mental disease, but admitted in cross-examination that she was passing through the stage of change of life, which could affect some women and cause them to suffer dizziness, 'muzziness' and irritability.

The judge left it open to the jury to bring in a 'Guilty but Insane' verdict, but pointed out that no medical evidence had been put forward on which they could base such a verdict. After only seventeen minutes, the jury brought in a verdict of 'Guilty', after which the judge passed the death sentence.

Annie Cook clung desperately to the last hope that her friend would be reprieved from the scaffold, and for several weeks she worked fourteen hours a day seeking support for a petition, but to no avail. No official appeal was mounted and Annie was Margaret's only visitor whilst in prison, none of her family making an appearance. On 11 January she had her last meeting with her friend. Margaret remained stoical to the end. 'You know the time tomorrow morning,' she said to a weeping Annie. 'Do me a favour and stand at the end of Kay Street in Rawtenstall. That's where we used to meet.'

'I shall be there,' said Annie, bursting into tears again. On her way out of the prison, the occasion became too much for her and she fainted. Some days after the execution, Annie received her friend's ring and cigarette lighter, which Margaret had expressly asked should be given to her.

During her period in prison, No.137 Bacup Road remained empty, although the landlord had several applications from people seeking accommodation. A twelve-hour canvass for a last-minute reprieve produced only 112 signatures, and one woman who was approached was said to have chased Annie Cook away with a broomstick.

The spot where Annie Cook had her vigil on the day of the execution. (A. Hayhurst)

The two small stone markers showing graves of executed criminals at Blackley cemetery. (A. Hayhurst)

On Wednesday, 12 January 1949, Albert Pierrepoint made one of his regular visits to Strangeways Gaol and dispatched Margaret Allen. Despite her wish to meet her end in male clothing, she was dressed in a blue smock and frock, supplied by the prison, and was the first woman to be hung since Charlotte Bryant in 1936, for the murder of her husband by poison.

A crowd of more than 300 people, mostly women and girls, waited outside the prison gates as execution time drew near. Mrs Violet Van der Elst, whose altercation with a bystander was hastily sorted by a constable, accompanied them. Mrs Van der Elst was a former scullery maid turned businesswoman, having developed 'Shavex', the first brushless shaving cream. This gave her a huge fortune, and, in 1937, she purchased Harlaxton Manor, an opulent 100-bedroom mansion in Lincolnshire. By the end of the 1930s she had become an active campaigner against capital punishment and was often to be seen outside prisons in her Rolls-Royce, with a loudspeaker horn fixed on top, which she used to address the crowd on hanging days, and to conduct the singing of hymns. She stood unsuccessfully three times as a prospective Labour MP but, by 1959, the upkeep of Harlaxton Manor and her campaigning had used up her entire fortune and she moved to a flat in Knightsbridge, dying penniless and friendless in 1965. She had, though, lived long enough to see the death penalty abolished.

Margaret Allen's body was buried inside the walls at Strangeways Prison in accordance with custom.

In 1993, following renovations at the prison, all the bodies of executed criminals (numbering approximately 100) were exhumed and the cremated remains were buried in two separate plots, numbered C2710 and C2711, in Blackley cemetery, Greater Manchester. Two stones, bearing the grave numbers and 'RIP', mark the spot, and from time to time small bunches of flowers appear, presumably left by relatives of those interred there.

14

THE SERIAL KILLER

Wigan, 1954/5

On Friday, 27 August 1954, a seven-year-old boy named Billy Mitchell, of Cross Street, Wigan, was playing with a friend, Alan Jones, on the bank of the nearby Leeds and Liverpool Canal. Jones was sitting on a low wall when he saw a man run up to his friend, seize him, and stab him in the chest with what looked like a penknife. Billy cried out in pain, which attracted the attention of two men who came running over and, realising what had happened, immediately ran off after the now fleeing attacker, shouting, 'All right son, we'll get him.'

Alan Jones jumped down on the other side of the wall and ran for help. Now alone and in tears, young Billy ran home and told his mother what had happened. The man, Billy said between sobs, was fair-haired and 'about as tall as Daddy', about 5ft 10in. He was blonde and was wearing a blue suit. The police were called and the young boy was examined and, fortunately for him, was found to have only a slight scratch. The two men who had chased after the attacker had not returned to the scene and the police immediately made it known that they were interested in interviewing them as soon as possible.

Barely half an hour later, the Wigan police were contacted again, this time by seventy-year-old Mr Joseph Mawdesley. He told them that he had been approached by a young man, Joseph Kelly, aged about thirty, who told him that there was a badly injured boy lying on some spare ground known as 'the Sands' on Miry Lane, formerly belonging to the Corporation, and that he thought that the boy was dying. The two men at once hurried to the spot and found eleven-year-old William Harmer, of Vere Street, Wigan, who had been repeatedly stabbed and was bleeding heavily. Mawdesley said, 'What's happened?', and the boy replied in a low voice, 'It's a man.' They were soon joined by Mawdesley's son-in-law, Edward Woods, who felt the boy's jersey and found it sticky with blood; the boy himself was now unconscious. A man named Hollinshead then came up and, recognising the young boy, told the others his

Police photograph of the murder scene in Miry Lane. (National Archives)

address. Kelly, who had originally come out to look for his young daughter, then left and Woods picked up the young boy, and, together with his father-in-law, took him to his home at 1 Vere Street, Wigan, only 400 yards away. Mrs Margaret Harmer, the boy's mother, was heavily pregnant with her sixth child, and when she saw her son was in a state of near collapse.

PC Gerald Ashurst was on motor patrol duty and received a message to go to Vere Street immediately. When he arrived, he found a number of people in the street and several more inside the house. Clearing all but the family out, he saw the young boy lying on a couch in a dishevelled state, his pullover saturated with blood. He started to render first aid, although he quickly decided that the boy was too close to death and decided to wait for the ambulance.

The boy's father, thirty-eight-year-old Samuel Harmer, who was then parading his greyhound at Woodhouse Lane Stadium, was hurriedly sent for and arrived just after the ambulance had taken William to hospital, where he died soon afterwards.

A post-mortem was carried out on Billy Harmer later in the day by Home Office Pathologist Dr George B. Manning. It revealed that there were eleven wounds on the boy's body. Meanwhile, more than a hundred policemen, some with metal detectors, combed the wasteland where Harmer had been found dying, looking for the murder weapon (possibly, they thought, a penknife). A woman, May Penman, who lived nearby at 75 Miry Lane, told the police that she had seen a stranger standing on the steps of the Crown Inn, wearing a light blue suit, age about twenty-five, and with light hair.

The police launched a house-to-house search and announced that they were looking for three men; the one who had told Joseph Mawdesley about William Harmer and the two men who had chased after Billy Mitchell's attacker. Within a short time, the Chief Constable had called in Scotland Yard to lead the investigation, and Superintendent Colin McDougall and Sergeant Harry Greaves arrived at Wigan police station. Meanwhile, police, armed with more than a dozen photos of blond men, toured the pubs and clubs of Wigan asking if any of the men had been in on the previous Friday night.

Soon, all three men wanted by the police had been found, and, after a reconstruction of the crime at the scene, they were interviewed by the Scotland Yard men. Joseph Kelly, known as 'Stiffy', was interviewed and then allowed to go, after describing how he had found William Harmer and had then passed on the information to Mawdesley. The other two men, who had chased Billy's attacker, were also interviewed and permitted to leave after satisfying the police that they had nothing to do with the assault on the boy.

Meanwhile, the dead boy's father was conducting his own one-man investigation. 'The police have all the facilities for investigation,' he told the *Evening Chronicle*, 'but I am doing the best I can to find my boy's killer. I think he lives somewhere in this area.'

Despite the number of detectives who were now being used in the search for Billy Harmer's killer, they found nothing to help them with the investigation and Mr Paul Foster, Wigan's Chief Constable, announced that, 'No early arrest is expected.' Throughout the North West, police forces were co-operating in the hunt for blood-stained clothing, visiting dozens of dyers' and cleaners' premises throughout Lancashire. The police were now also considering the possibility that young Harmer had been attacked somewhere else and had either staggered or been dragged to where he was found. A particularly puzzling element was the absence of blood at the crime scene. Disused premises near the murder scene, known to the local children as 'the haunted mill', received special scrutiny, as Alan Jones said that the attacker had come from that direction.

Additional police were brought in, including Detective Chief Superintendent C. Lindsay, Head of the County CID, and Detective Chief Inspector W. Roberts, who had led the investigation into another recent child-stabbing, that of six-year-old Wilfred Schofield of Higher Ince, near Wigan, who had been found dead, with five stab wounds, on spare ground 500 yards from his home on 18 June. No one had been caught for this crime, although nine-year-old Thomas Bamber had admitted that he and two other lads had been playing with Wilfred that evening when the boy had been hurt with a knife; it was apparently he, Bamber, who had been holding it. Later, he was to retract his statement, saying that he was with his grandfather elsewhere at the time. In the event, the coroner afterwards recorded a verdict of 'Misadventure'.

Amongst the suspects that the police still wished to interview was a man who had telephoned Kemsley Newspapers, in Manchester, on the night of the murder, nearly an hour before the boy was killed. He said that a missing boy had been found, believed murdered. Another man, who claimed to be a journalist, went into a Wigan public house and showed round a photograph of barmaid Eunice Clements, murdered twelve years ago at Newtown near Wigan. 'They didn't find the murderer and they won't find the boy's,' he told people in the bar. Weeks went by and although the police continued to work diligently in their quest for Billy Harmer's murderer, the trail went cold and eventually the Scotland Yard detectives returned to London and the operation slowly wound down.

On Monday, 11 April 1955, at 9.40 p.m., the body of ten-year-old Norman Yates was found by Mr James Jones in Back Hope Street, Ince. Jones had been listening to the radio when he heard a scream and, for a moment, thought that it had come from his four-year-old daughter, Doris. Shouting to a man to assist him, he heard another scream and ran towards it, discovering the body of Norman Yates lying in a pool of blood. He had been stabbed four times, and on arrival at Wigan Infirmary was pronounced dead. Young Norman had been on an errand to fetch some sugar from his aunt's house in Hope Street.

The post-mortem, conducted by Dr Manning, disclosed that the boy had been found fully clothed, but his trousers had been pulled down and the fly buttons torn off. He had been stabbed four times – on the neck, chest and lower body – and cause of death was haemorrhage from an incised wound in the neck. The murder weapon was thought to be a small, pointed instrument.

A man who was seen in the vicinity at the time was described as being 'approximately twenty-three years old, about 5ft 3in to 5ft 4in in height, slim build, with

Back Hope Street, Ince. (National Archives)

fairly long blond hair brushed straight back and clean shaven.' The police were immediately thick on the ground, conducting house-to-house searches, stopping traffic to ask drivers if they had given a lift to a man resembling the wanted man's description, and watching the railways. Drains around the scene of the crime were scooped out in a search for the weapon and a sharp-pointed paint scraper found in a telephone box about a mile from the scene was taken to Lower Ince police station. This was dismissed by the police as having no connection with the murder; they were still convinced that the weapon was likely to have been a small penknife.

A notice was flashed on cinema screens within a seven-mile radius of the Wigan area:

> Two boys have already been stabbed to death, your help may prevent another boy being murdered. The police are interested in interviewing a slim man with blond hair, who has a habit of rubbing his hands together. If you know this man or can give any information, tell the police.

It was also announced that a hairstylist was preparing several samples of hair, ranging from light brown to very blond, for witnesses to compare. It was still puzzling the police how the boy could have been stabbed within sight of a row of houses, with the killer getting clean away.

The breakthrough came when a trawl of the local dry-cleaning shops (an attempt to find men who had brought bloodstained clothing in for cleaning) revealed Norman William Green, a twenty-five-year-old corn-grinder of Hallgate, Wigan. He had taken in a blue, two-piece suit and was interviewed by PC John Wareing, who noticed particularly that Green's hair was practically white. Green explained to the constable why he had decided to have his suit cleaned and, for the moment, his reply was placed with all the others.

On Friday 15 April, Inspector Tom Edmondson, together with Detective Sergeant Parkinson, pulled up outside the offices of Charlson & Son, Corn Grinders of Dawber Street, Wigan, and asked to see Norman Green. Green was called to the manager's office, where the two policemen were waiting to ask him about his movements on the day of the murder. Green appeared quite at ease as he answered, 'I went out for a paper about 7 o'clock in the evening and then had a walk round Wigan. I then went home about half past eight.' At this point, Green hesitated and Edmondson asked, 'Did you stay in your house for the remainder of the night?' Green paused, before answering, 'No, I went out again to the Market Square and had a drink at the Bath Springs pub. I then walked around the town and got home just after ten o'clock. I never went to Ince that night.'

'Where did you go after you left the Bath Springs?' asked Edmondson.

'I went along Crompton Street, past the Ritz, to the toilets in Millgate and then stood in front of the Hippodrome and got home just after ten.'

'How did you know the time?' quizzed the detective.

Norman Green. (Author's Collection)

'I was wearing this,' said Green, reaching into his shirt pocket and pulling out a chromium-plated wristwatch with a leather strap.

'Where do you usually wear that?'

'On my left wrist,' replied Green.

Edmondson leaned forward and stared at the young man. 'You answer the description of a man seen in the Railway Hotel, Lower Ince, around 9 p.m.' Green looked surprised. 'It wasn't me,' he said. 'I've already told you, I never went near Ince on Easter Monday.'

'Did you know that the police were anxious to interview a man of your description?' persisted Edmondson.

'I did not want any trouble, that's why I did not come forward.'

The detective drew in a deep breath. 'I am not satisfied with your explanation,' he began and Green blurted out, 'Oh, I remember now. I did go in the Railway, but I've nothing to do with that boy.'

Carefully, Edmondson told Green that he was being arrested on a charge of murder, and he was taken to Lower Ince police station, where he was interviewed further by the formidable trio of Chief Superintendent Cecil Lindsay, who had returned from London, Chief Inspector Riley and Inspector Parkinson.

Chief Superintendent Lindsay took up the questioning. 'When you were first seen by the Detective Sergeant this afternoon, did you deny having been in the Railway Inn on Easter Monday night?'

'Yes,' replied Green, 'but I told the truth after.'

'Were you aware that the police were looking for a blond man in the vicinity of the Railway Inn?'

'Yes, but there's more blonds than me,' protested Green.

'I would like to take a sample of your hair,' said the senior policeman.

'Alright, as long as you don't spoil it,' Green said. 'The chaps at work have been razzing me about being blond, saying that the cops would come for me and that I'd get the rope.'

'Why didn't you come forward, then?' questioned Lindsay.

'Because I'd nothing to do with it. I'm not the type you're looking for.'

'What type do you think we are looking for?' asked Lindsay.

'Like Straffen,' came the reply. (John Thomas Straffen was a twenty-two-year-old child-murderer, who escaped from Broadmoor and killed again in 1951.)

'What do you know about Straffen?' Lindsay pressed.

'I read about him. He killed two little kids and they didn't hang him. Didn't they send him to an asylum?'

Green carried on talking, this time about his mother, and his brother and sister, repeating that he had had nothing to do with the murder of Norman Yates. 'Do I look like one who would do that?' he exclaimed. 'I go to the Mission a lot. I was at one with my brother at Chorley last Friday.'

The Chief Superintendent tried another tack. 'Do you own a knife?' he asked.

'No, I never carry a penknife,' came the reply.

'I asked you if you had a knife. I never mentioned a penknife.'

'They say he was stabbed with a penknife,' Green responded. 'I have a jack-knife at work, but I never carry it. I get the urge to drink beer sometimes,' he went on lamely, 'but I fight against it. Same with cigarettes.'

Meanwhile, Inspector Edmondson had been to Green's home at 102 Hallgate, Wigan, from where he took away a blue jacket, a pair of matching trousers and a pair of brown shoes. Green later admitted that he had been wearing that outfit on the night of Norman Yates' murder. Once again, Green was cautioned and he replied, 'I am very sorry and I am sorry for his mother. I hope she forgives me for what I have done.'

Later, Green was taken to his employer's factory, where the police took possession of a jack-knife found on his workbench. Green then indicated a sack full of corn and said, 'This is the one.' Inside was a penknife. Green said, 'That's the knife. I think there will be blood on it.'

Norman Green's knife was found inside one of these sacks. (National Archives)

'Can you account for it?' said Lindsay.

'I got an urge to do it.' Green was sobbing now. 'I fight against it, but it's no use.' Green then made the following statement:

> Most of the things I told you before are lies and I wish to tell the truth. I left home at 8 p.m. and went to the Bath Springs for a drink of beer, then I caught a bus to the Old Hall and had a drink there. Then I went to the Walmsley and about 9 p.m. I went in the Railway after talking to a bloke. I came out of the Railway and saw a little boy coming along the street and I said, 'Can you give me a drink of water?' He said, 'Yes, you can have one at my mother's,' and we walked up an entry towards the back of some houses. We went across the street and I killed him there ... I stabbed him four times with the weapon I had. Then I walked to Frog Lane and went home ... I am sorry for all the trouble I have brought on my mother and hope she'll forgive me and forgive my father for drowning himself at North Shields. I have been wicked and deserve the worst punishment.

Green was then locked up, and at Wigan Petty Sessions he pleaded 'Not Guilty'. Later, he made another statement, referring to the murder of Billy Harmer.

> I remember the murder down Prescot Street last August, because I did it. I went down the canal bank and saw a boy and went to him to try and kill him, but he screamed and ran down the canal bank. I went down Miry Lane and went in a pub for a drink. Later, about 9.30 p.m., I walked towards Prescott Street, when a voice from the spare ground asked me if I was looking for someone. It was the boy, William Harmer. I killed him with a knife, which I later threw away.

Enquiries were made as to Green's background, and it transpired that his real name was McLean, after his father, John. His father's marriage to Green's mother had broken up fifteen years before and Norman had adopted her surname when she married again. He was evacuated during the war, finally leaving school on 24 July 1943 to start work as a milk-delivery boy with Wigan Co-op. In July 1947, after taking his medical for the forces and being adjudged Grade 2, he opted to go down the pit rather than go into the army, but left of his own accord in November 1950. His final medical had rated him as Grade 3, due to a hernia and a weak right eye. The report stated that he was emotionally unstable, nervous and had a slight stammer.

Since July 1951, he had been working at Charlson's. There they considered him to be excellent at his job; conscientious, dependable and a good timekeeper. His mother had not fared so well though. Her second husband, John Thomas Green, was addicted to heavy drinking and had fifty-four court appearances between February 1911 and January 1950. She left him on several occasions and he later left her to live with another woman. The recalcitrant husband was found drowned in the River Tyne on 28 March 1950.

Enquiries also disclosed that Norman Green had enjoyed fairly good health and had never been treated for a serious complaint. His mother, however, insisted that

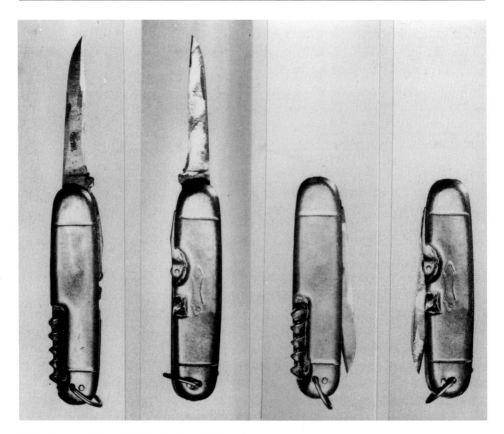

Police pictures of Green's knife. (National Archives)

for the past two years her son had been suffering from violent headaches and whilst there was no evidence of insanity on his mother's side, there was on the father's.

The trial, before Mr Justice Oliver, in which Green was accused of the single murder of Norman Yates (despite Green's written confessions), lasted five days. Green's defence was one of insanity. Dr Isaac Frost, consulting psychiatrist for the Liverpool Hospital Board, said that during the hearing he had had four interviews with the condemned man and considered that at the time he stabbed Norman Yates, he was suffering from temporal lobe epilepsy.

The judge leaned forward. 'You are not suggesting he is mad now?'

'I do, my Lord. I regard him as certifiable now.' Dr Frost also said that Green had told him that he had been thinking about killing people since the age of fourteen, but that he had fought against it.

'So he knew that it was wrong?' asked the judge, and Dr Frost had to agree. A point that might have been in Green's favour was thus turned against him by the judge's intervention.

A second defence witness, Dr John Raymond Murray, told the court that an uncle of the accused was an inmate of St George's Mental Hospital, Morpeth, and suffered from delusional insanity. A half-brother of the accused also showed signs of violent activity and was suffering from schizophrenia. Mrs Frances Hill, wife of the licensee of the Railway Inn, Lower Ince, gave evidence that she had seen a stranger come into the pub on Easter Monday with exceptionally light hair. 'I had never seen hair so light before,' she told the court, 'but there was nothing unusual about his manner.' Several other witnesses were also able to describe a man with very blond hair near the Railway Hotel on the night of the murder. One noticed that the man had a wristlet watch, 'that looked like silver'.

Summing up, Mr Justice Oliver said that there could be no doubt that the man in the dock had committed the murder. The questions the members of the jury had to ask themselves were, did the accused know what he was doing, and, supposing he knew he was killing a child, did he know that he was doing wrong?

After four hours of deliberation, the jury returned to ask the judge for assistance on the 'balance of probabilities', a phrase that the judge had used in his summing up. Having received the judge's explanation, the jury then retired again; on returning they found themselves in no doubt that Green was guilty of the death of Norman Yates, and was also sane at the time.

The judge passed the sentence of death without further ado. Green's mother and his brother were not in the courtroom to hear the verdict and sentence; they were sitting in a corridor in another part of the building, having been unable to face the tension whilst the jury were out. The charge of murder in respect of William Harmer was ordered to lie on file and not to be taken forward without permission of the court.

There was no public appeal, the defence contenting themselves with a last-minute plea to the Home Secretary – this had no effect though. On 27 July 1955, about thirty onlookers, mainly women, waited outside the main gate of Walton Gaol, Liverpool for the execution notice to be posted. Albert Pierrepoint and his assistant, Robert Stewart, had arrived at the prison the previous afternoon and their arrangements went without a hitch. At her home in Hallgate, Green's mother sat quietly in the back kitchen, eyes closed in prayer as the dreadful hour approached. None of the family was at the prison.

A curious feature of the case was that Green, with his almost albino hair colouring (his nickname amongst his workmates was 'Snowball'), seemed to have taken no precautions at all against being recognised. There were also strong suspicions that he had been involved in the death, by stabbing, of six-year-old William Schofield.

Note: Despite strenuous attempts by the author to obtain embargoed files at the National Archives, under the Freedom of Information Act, access to files MEPO 2/9551 and ASSI 86/111 were refused and these remain unavailable to the public.

BIBLIOGRAPHY

1. SUSPICIOUS DEATH IN THE WORKHOUSE

Atholl, J., *The Reluctant* Hangman (John Long, 1956)
Bailey, B., *Hangman* (True Crime, 1993)
Berry, J., *My Experiences as an Executioner* (Percy Lund & Co. 1900)
Doughty, J., *The Rochdale Hangman* (Jade Publishing, 1998)
Evans, S.P., *Executioner: The Chronicles of James Berry* (Sutton, 2004)
National Archives: ASSI 52/9

2. A MYSTERIOUS STRANGER

Greenhalgh, S., *Foul Deeds and Suspicious Deaths in Blackburn* (Wharncliffe, 2002)
Johnson, K., *Chilling True Tales of Old Lancashire* (Sigma, 1996)
National Archives: ASSI 52/1, HO 144/18846, PCOM 8/41

3. THE HORROR UPSTAIRS

Bruce, A., *Billington: Victorian Executioner* (The History Press, 2009)
National Archives: ASSI 52/24

4. THE HANGMAN PASSING BY

Pierrepoint, A., *Executioner Pierrepoint* (Harrap, 1974)
National Archives: ASSI 52/58

5. 'I'LL DO IT! I'LL DO IT!'

National Archives: ASSI 52/88

6. 'There is None Like Alice to Me'

National Archives: ASSI 52/184

7. Death on the Dunes

Marjoribanks, E., *Life of Sir Edward Marshall Hall* (Victor Gollancz, 1929)
National Archives: ASSI 52/309, HO 144/1619

8. Fourpence for Ice Cream

National Archives: ASSI 52/356, HO 144/4116, PCOM 8/76

9. 'We Have Both Gone to Mother'

National Archives: ASSI 52/375, PCOM 8/167

10. A Village Tragedy

National Archives: ASSI 52/522, CRIM 1/1352, DPP 2/878, HO 144/21565, HO 144/21639, PCOM 9/895 (freed under the Freedom of Information Act)

11. Murder in the Park

National Archives: ASSI 52/535, DPP 2/950, DPP 2/988, PCOM 9/918, HO 144/21657

12. Death of a Pawnbroker

Eddleston, J.J., *Murderous Manchester* (Breedon Books, 1997)
National Archives: ASSI 52/581, PCOM 9/707, HO 144/22854, DPP 2/1493, ASSI 86/6 (freed under Freedom of Information Act)

13. 'In One of my Funny Moods'

Van der Elst, V., *On The Gallows* (The Doge Press, 1937)
National Archives: HO 45/23935, ASSI 52/629, ASSI 86/21 (freed under the Freedom of Information Act)

14. The Serial Killer

National Archives: ASSI 52/838, PCOM 9/2083, DPP 2/2432

NEWSPAPERS

Blackburn Times
Blackburn Weekly Telegraph
Daily Dispatch
Daily Express
Daily Post
Daily Telegraph
Darwen News
Empire News
Huddersfield Daily Chronicle
Liverpool Daily Post
Liverpool Echo
Liverpool Mercury
Manchester Courier
Manchester Evening Chronicle
Manchester Evening News
Manchester Guardian
Northern Evening Telegraph
Preston Guardian
Rochdale Observer
Salford Reporter
Southport Visitor
The Globe
The Star
The Times

GENERAL READING

Eddlestone, J.J., *The Encyclopaedia of Executions* (John Blake, 2002)
Fielding, S., *Pierrepoint: A Family of Executioners* (John Blake, 2006)
Fielding, S., *The Executioner's Bible* (John Blake, 2007)

INDEX

Other titles published by The History Press

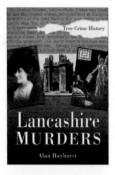

Lancashire Murders

ALAN HAYHURST

The chilling cases covered here record the county's most fascinating but least known crimes, as well as famous murders that gripped not just Lancashire but the whole nation. From the infamous Drs Ruxton and Clements who saw off five wives between them, to Blackpool's Louisa Merrifield, whose loose tongue was undoubtedly her downfall, this is a collection of the most dramatic and interesting criminal cases from the area. *Lancashire Murders* is a unique re-examination of the darker side of the county's past.

978 0 7509 3693 4

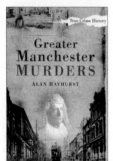

Greater Manchester Murders

ALAN HAYHURST

Contained within these pages you will find the stories behind some of the most notorious murders in the history of Greater Manchester: the case of cat burglar Charlie Peace, who killed 20-year-old PC Nicholas Cook in Seymour Grove; the sad tale of William Robert Taylor, whose young daughter was killed in a boiler explosion and who later murdered a bailiff as well as his three remaining children; and John Jackson, who escaped from Strangeways Gaol by killing a prison warder.

978 0 7509 5091 6

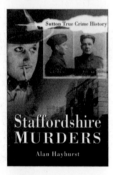

Staffordshire Murders

ALAN HAYHURST

Staffordshire Murders brings together shocking tales that made headline news throughout the nation as well as the county. They include a murder on the canal, a tale of infanticide, a chauffeur's revenge story and much more. Alan Hayhurst has spent many hours visiting the scenes detailed in this book, as well as researching original documents. His well-illustrated and enthralling text will appeal to all who are interested in the shady side of Staffordshire's history.

978 0 7509 4706 0

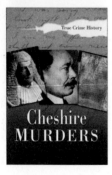

Chesire Murders

ALAN HAYHURST

Some of the gruesome cases in this book are better known than others, such as the inexplicable shooting of his wife and two daughters by Lock Ah Tam in 1926. Others are less well known, including the mysterious murder of Mary Malpas in 1835 and the crime of Frederick George Wood in Bramhall in 1922, while few outside the town have ever heard the tale of the 'Congleton Cannibal'. The murders and mysteries featured here are sure to grip true crime enthusiasts everywhere.

978 0 7509 4076 4

Visit our website and discover thousands of other History Press books.

www.thehistorypress.co.uk